Spotlight Poets

PORTRAITS OF PASSION

Edited by

Steve Twelvetree & Kelly Deacon

First published in Great Britain in 2000 by
SPOTLIGHT POETS
Remus House, Coltsfoot Drive,
Woodston,
Peterborough, PE2 9JX
Telephone (01733) 898102
Fax (01733) 313524

All Rights Reserved

Copyright Contributors 1999

SB ISBN 1 84077 036 8

FOREWORD

As a nation of poetry writers and lovers, many of us are still surprisingly reluctant to go out and actually buy the books we cherish so much. Often when searching out the work of newer and less known authors it becomes a near impossible mission to track down the sort of books you require. In an effort to break away from the endless clutter of seemingly unrelated poems from authors we know nothing or little about; Spotlight Poets has opened up a doorway to something quite special.

'Portraits Of Passion' is a collection of poems to be cherished forever; featuring the work of twelve captivating poets each with a selection of their very best work. Placing that alongside their own personal profile gives a complete feel for the way each author works, allowing for a clearer idea of the true feelings and reasoning behind the poems.

The poems and poets have been chosen and presented in a complementary anthology that offers a variety of ideals and ideas, capable of moving the heart, mind and soul of the reader.

Steve Twelvetree & Kelly Deacon

CONTENTS

Rosemary Orr		1
	Stranger	2
	Inspirational Flowers	3
	November Sun	4
	Anemones	4
	Winter Blues	5
	Snowdrops At Turvey	6
	It Is . . .	7
	Sacred Space	8
	November Rain	9
	Kasifa At Namuganga, Uganda	10
	East Indian Ecstasy	11
	On Mother's Day	12
	December Twilight At Turvey	12
Jacki Larcombe		13
	Homecoming	14
	Waiting	15
	The Girl	16
	Somnolent Crescent Moon	17
	A June Storm	18
	The Haunted Wood	19
	God	20
	Words Are Just	21
	Dawn	22
	Sunset At Sea	23
	Today	24
Stan McKerron		25
	Circle Of Life	26
Yvonne Marie Beattie		34
	Feelings	35
	A Plea For Justice	36
	Springtime	36
	The Tunnel Of Despair	37

	The Overwhelming Shadows	38
	Aspects Of Love	39
	Anger	40
	Just For You	41
	The Swift Thief	42
	Always Friends	42
	My Little Treasure	43
	A Lament For Them All	44
Terry Ireland		45
	Shoes	46
	Sunday Morning, Post Waltzing Weasel	47
	November 1993	48
	Withernwick, Now	49
	Post Cod War Blues, November 1991	50
	Girl	51
	Derbyshire	52
	Pigeons	52
	Creation	53
	Small Steps	54
	Fingers	54
Ann Grimwood		55
	Ann's Poem	56
	I'll Share Your Burden	56
	Mirror Mirror	57
	A Burning	57
	It's My Decision	58
	Don't Worry	59
	To Let You Know	59
	By Royal Appointment	60
	The Morning After	60
	My Precious Baby	61
	I'm No Different	61
	Child Abuse - The Child's Story	62
	A New Life Is Born	63

	It's Time To Come Home	64
	The Lost Soul	64
Maria Pelengaris		65
	Reality	66
	For You	67
	A Moment In Time	68
	Now That I Love You	68
	Black Dream, Black Day	69
	All I Remember	70
	The Incubation Period	71
	Blood Sisters	72
	Journey On	73
	Taj Mahal	74
	Six O'Clock	75
Marcella Pellow		76
	Good Friday	77
	Easter	77
	Good Friday	78
	Thankfulness	78
	To Our King Emmanuel	79
	The Sea	79
	A Prayer for Grace	80
	For My Father	80
	Prayers Morn And Night	81
	Spring Son	81
	Spring In Cornwall	82
	For The Milkman	82
	Garden In May	83
	Christmas	83
	'Carloose' (Once My Home)	84
Trudy Lapinskis		85
	My Brother Garry	86
	Jackie	87
	Mother Teresa	88
	Dr Wedley	89

	Time	89
	NHS	90
	A Child Of War	91
	Remembrance Day	92
	Pain	93
	With Thanks	94
	Why Should We Be So Scared Of The Dark?	95
Joanna L Hammond		96
	A Summer's Afternoon	97
	Love Is . . .	97
	Untitled	98
	A Haze Of Memory	99
	An Eternal Ocean Dream	100
	Pain	101
	Untitled	102
	One Day	103
	Lonely	104
Mick Webster		105
	The Sky Is Falling	106
	Heaven's Echo	106
	Summer's Brief Song	107
	Dark Before Dawn	107
	Daddy's Girl	108
	Mother And Daughter	108
	Painful Goodbyes	109
	A House Filled With Love	110
	Ten Paces At Dawn	110
	A Penny For Your Thoughts	111
	Chances Are	112
	Broken Dreams	112
	Joy Or Shame?	113
	Rhapsody Of My Eyes	114
	Why?	114
	Where Lies The Blame?	115

Tina Rooney 116
Oh What A Bloody War! 117
Shining Light 118
Sunrise, Sunset 119
Kosovo Child 120
Jill Dando 121
Global Warming 122
Diana, Princess Of Wales 123
Millennium 124

Rosemary Orr

I was born in Birmingham on Christmas Day 1949. I was bandy-legged and club footed, a condition known as spastic paraplegia but after an operation I was at last able to walk at two years old. My parents sent me to normal schools but I was slow to write at first because of my disability and temporarily fell further behind because I was overcome by grief when my mother died just after my 13th birthday. However I had and still have, a strong belief in God and helped by a school teacher who taught RE, and nurtured by my church, I eventually went to Lancaster University to read Religious Studies where I gained a BA upper second class honours degree in 1971.

After that I suffered further trauma trying to do further study, care for my father, and locked in by buried grief for my mother, and this resulted in a series of nervous breakdowns. However I recovered from these and after the first, met my husband to be, to whom I have been happily married for 26 years. He too has a mental health problem: he is manic depressive and I am schizophrenic. The down-side of this relationship is that because of our health problems, we have been unable to care for our son and he finds it difficult to acknowledge us, hence the poems *Stranger* and *On Mother's Day*. Sometimes in all this, it has been difficult to make sense of this but I take strength from my faith in Jesus who was also human and suffered, and I am nurtured by the love of my husband and by regular visits to Turvey Abbey, where the Benedictine Nuns offer unlimited love and hospitality.

At the age of 15 I won a consolation prize in a national essay competition on the theme of my favourite haunts in the countryside, fields and parks. Throughout my life I have been drawn to themes connected with nature and spirituality and find freedom and joy in such self-expression, which renews my hope and gives me the energy to go forward on my uniquely personal pilgrimage.

I owe thanks to the mental health charity SANE who gave me a grant to begin writing. Also to University Centre Northampton Writing Group run by Sally Spedding. Both Sally and all the members of this group are a constant help and inspiration. I also am nourished by Chameleon Writers Co-op who meet monthly at NUTRAC in Northampton, particularly their Facilitator Zorina Ishmail Bibby. Thanks also go to the editors at Remus House for their steady encouragement.

STRANGER

I only glimpsed you in silhouette, in that damp twilight.
You looked intent and serious
Yet your hair was longer and flyaway
So perhaps you sought after a long-lost youth.

I recalled your infancy, remembering that boy in blue
With ruffled golden hair
Unconventional with strong ideals
A will firm and unswerving.

But I saw a different side of you that evening.
No signs of recognition in your eyes,
Clad in heavy coat and scarf
Hands hid layered in garments.

'I'm me and I don't want you.'
You seemed to be saying.
Were you depressed or was that
A misconception?

One breath and you'd moved on
Lost amongst the shadows.
Perhaps you strove still, but in my world,
You were eclipsed into the shades of night.

INSPIRATIONAL FLOWERS

A cascade of Chrysanthemums.
An autumnal rainbow.
Pale white, subtle salmon,
And buttercup-yellow.
Also murmuring Michaelmas Daisies.

I could not bear to unpack you,
Unfold the rose bow.
You were special
Inspirational flowers.

A glorious surprise.
Finally I placed
Each steam carefully
In a crystal vase.
Then I looked again.

What pride
What confidence
You gave me.
Your leaves
Like fronds of seaweed
Frolicking.

In a few weeks
You will be gone
So I encapsulate
Your memory
And all who encourage me.

Live then my Inspirational Flowers!

NOVEMBER SUN

I almost am bewitched
Into thinking it's midsummer,
Slats of strong sunlight everywhere.

People walk briskly,
Talk animatedly,
Laugh contentedly.

Although I am in open air,
Buildings line the market square,
I scan the sky to source the golden glow.

No it's not June.
The sunlight exists it seems
Apart from the sun

But then I walk up steps,
There is a sweep of sky
Low down I catch the sun

Soon to vanish beneath the horizon,
Leaving only rosehips rotting,
Betraying the true season.

ANEMONES

Born of wind and sea
You were loved by my mother,
Purple, pink and white, your thick stems
Bend outward in clumsy supplication.

Your petals reach out
From dark bulbous stamens,
Secretive, hard and surreal.
Around these a frond of green
Fragile like cut parsley.

Can I pass through
Your hidden centre?
Or must I wait for you to reveal
Your treasurers from this frozen posture?

I gaze on,
Waiting for a metamorphosis,
A long expected sea change,
From your womb from where you came
Born of wind and sea.

WINTER BLUES

Today is a particularly bleak day.
My husband is in the throes of depression,
I, too, am feeling down.

Winter is in the ascendant.
The weather may be mild,
But in my heart there is bitter chill.

I feel frustrated in this marriage
Trapped and entombed,
I wait for someone to roll the stone away.

But it is still Good Friday for me
And life seems like a crucifixion
Over and over again.

The sun is still eclipsed.
I sense sorrow and mourning,
I do not know if the sun will rise again.

I try to look forward,
Anticipating new relationships,
Consolidating old bonds.

Nevertheless today is still a particularly bleak day.

SNOWDROPS AT TURVEY

Tiny snowdrops clustered together
A unison of white petals
Protecting each and all

From the mellow westerly wind
Blowing its bellows onwards
Bound as if captive inside an earth tunnel.

The snowdrops triumph warmed
By February sun, shadowed
By a larger cluster of monastic buildings.

Near the higgledy-piggledy path
They rock gently to the rhythm of
Overhead firs solemn sentinels in sympathy

With their larger sisters
In habits of white, silently
Being themselves exposed

To the greater glory of God
A unity of holy work and prayer
Maybe a cloister of Benedictine snowdrops

Held and cherished in his love
Earthed in this quiet woodland retreat
Just tiny snowdrops clustered together.

IT IS...

It is going out on a bright winter's morning
Expecting to be warmed by the sun and instead feeling
A sharp chill racing through my bones.

It is looking at the blue-green water sensing
Warmth and wet and then slowly swimming
A sense of being alive from head to toes.

It is waiting in the coffee bar looking
For half-expected friends and then meeting
A promise fulfilled as we exchanged glances.

It is standing on the lonely road in the darkening
Twilight. The bus will come I say and then hearing
A roar of its engine while its headlight gleams

It is being in the kitchen, cooking smells wafting,
Hungry, yet in my mind enjoying and eating,
A certainty of well-being it seems.

It is climbing into bed under the duvet clutching
The hot water bottle and then shivering
As hoped for warmth slowly penetrates.

It is drifting into sleep and peacefully dreaming
Finding green slopes and over white beaches roaming
Immersed in summer sun and breaking sea waves.

SACRED SPACE

Scatterings of mole earth
Adorn the uncut lawn,
With its buttercup patches,
Daisies and untidy sunlight

In Turvey chapel order prevails.
Christ in risen splendour
Stands supreme arms uplifted
A charism of joy.

Pale pink and red amaryllis
Echo his ecstasy,
While bread is broken,
Blood-red wine outpoured.

Later in the Easter Garden
I hear a cock crow,
Three wooden crosses rise up
Alongside an empty tomb.

Unlike Peter in Galilee
I betray not the moment,
Water iris on sunken pond
Draws dithering dragonflies.

Near the pointed stone arches,
Beneath latticed window
In her white habit sits a sister,
Relishing the cool shade.

I surmise not the secrets
Of her Benedictine seclusion
But cherish high summer, savouring
Transient but sublime sacred space.

NOVEMBER RAIN

Dreary drip dripping of grey rain.
Everywhere is sodden with wet.
People huddle together,
Shrouded in winter coats,
Hidden by umbrellas.
Their voices drowned
By hissing trees
and drenching water.

I hurry along treading
Down slippery autumn leaves
Decomposing underfoot.
Once home I drink hot soup.
Relentless is the gloom
Through rain-splattered windows
But I am warm now.
I shut my eyes and hear
The trickle of water.
Suddenly I float on downy grass
Summer has come and the mountain steam
Cascades down the green sunny valley.

Then I open my eyes and once more
I see the dreary drip dripping of grey November rain
Winter bleakness is come with a vengeance.

KASIFA AT NAMUGANGA, UGANDA

The rains have come and gone
Today the road is dusty dry.
Near trees and bushes heavy with green,
You stand proud and erect

Clothed in purple and as I see you
Your solemnity becomes smiles
Running forward you say, 'Welcome,
Mrs Rosemary,' and I, 'Hullo Kasifa.'

We hug one another
I see your house made of burnt bricks,
The television where you saw
Clinton on his Ugandan State visit.

Then we go to the storehouse where
Harvest of Soya beans, maize,
Sweet potato and coffee are stored
With the dried fish from the market

'Come and see our goats and sheep'
An African boy appears carrying
A sheep, led by him we reach the compound
While his sister carries water for all to drink.

Later we drive along the track
To Namuganga School where we rush
Into the new toilet flush with ochre paint
Then inside the primary classroom.

It is the weekend and the site is deserted.
The sun is setting casting golden shadows
Over the iron sheets of the school roof.
Kasifa and I hug again.

Then we look into each other's eyes
Hers brown as hazel, mine salt sea-blue.
I fix my present, a tiny gold cross,
Around her neck, we cling, loose

Then I must be gone into another world,
But perhaps we are not so far apart,
For where there is food and fun
Smiles are laughter, we are forever one.

EAST INDIAN ECSTASY

Aroused I raise my zarf, this rich ornament
Containing my coffee cup, cappuccino hot
Brim full, mouth luxuriating, while sitting
In the shade of the Sundari tree.

Elephants eating eddish, their rich pasture
Mowed once, now being slowly digested,
Avoid fragile pelitic rock baked
In East Indian sun. In my other hand

I clasp my sea ear and in its depths
I sense a gentle zither echoing
Jovial delight, delicately defining,
My slow awakening from a midday siesta.

On Mother's Day

On Mother's Day the children send cards
And flowers to their mothers.

I, though fertile, am only a mother in name,
A throwaway label the writing obscured.

All my bitter-sweet memories are long past
Swept on the landfill site never retrieved.

My son will never send a card or present
He does not want to know me.

He does not want to admit he is mine.
On Mother's Day we are apart and estranged.

This child sends flowers and cards to another mother
Leaving me alone to weep.

December Twilight At Turvey

Ivy cloaks the dry stone wall.
Quiet birdsong emerges from the trees
Whose branches move like animated skeletons.
Above the hum of traffic their gentle tapping,
Dull and mysterious, like the fading grey light.

I observe this from my room
On a bleak December day.
My desk lamp a honey glow.
My room a warm haven,
From the outdoor chill,
Where tiny snowflakes fall
Welcoming the night.

JACKI LARCOMBE

I have been writing poetry since I was about seventeen. I write poetry because somehow the written word best reflects and conveys depth of feeling and expression. Most of my poetry reflects some aspect of my life so my subject matter varies from the countryside to philosophical ideas on life and love, and being alone. I do write on happier subjects, but my forte is non rhyming reflections on life.

I was brought up in Canada so some of my poetry reflects that time in my life. Since I have been back in England I have married and had four children, although now I am a single parent, and three of my children are adults. I have always lived in the country so again my poetry may reflect that lifestyle. I am influenced by what I read to a certain extent. Certainly reading gives me a better grasp of the psyche of human nature. I love writers like Mary Wesley, Joanna Trollop, Jeffrey Archer, James Mitchener to name but a few. One of my own ambitions is to write a novel, but I'm not quite ready yet. I also want to learn to speak Spanish and live on a boat.

I spend a great deal of time working on the completion of my degree in History and History of ideas. Over the years I have attended evening classes, Saturday schools and day classes in my drive to get my degree and I have enjoyed every minute of it. I have met lots of interesting people and made many new friends. Currently I am working on a History dissertation involving the media and British Fascism. I will graduate in June 2000 with a BA Hons, so that will mean party time.

HOMECOMING

He sat at dusk on the outcrop,
black against the grey sky,
sheathed in misery, alone
while rain spat at him, stretching to
touch his ageing face concealed
by the hunch of his shoulders.
So he had sat night after night,
mumbled prayers on his lips,
unaware of the weather that could
not reach him where he sat, immobile,
marked by the torments of time.
Briefly his cigarette glowed,
a spark of red in the night sky,
then as quickly died while
night clouds grew thick around
him, and still he waited,
silent, unmoving in the growing
storm that was not as great as the
one that raged within his heart.
Far off a light shone on the horizon,
looming larger as it took on
shape and form, and somewhere
laughter echoed and a lazy voice
answered in return.
He stood quickly, straining his eyes
out to sea, moonlight turning
his hair to ghostly white.
Shadows of pain vanished, tears
blurred his old eyes and a smile
lingered at his moustached mouth,
his head cocked, listening, watching,
as the fishing boat grated at last onto
silvered sand, dark shapes falling and
tumbling in relief in the moonlight.

Voices greeting, calling, hands slipping
into his, arms of love wrapping him
close to his first born, his son.
Days of torment over, of waiting
and weeping was done, for the great
heaving sea had once again given
him back his son - this time.

WAITING

    I am waiting for darkness to come
      and reveal your face to me
        in the passing of my dreams.
    In the shadows I hear your voice
      from the echoes of my mind,
    and I remember your laughter
     and the warmth of your eyes.
    Then gently with your passing
       come other memories
   of the years we shared as one
    and the children we bore.
  Yet only in the dark of my sleep
    can I relive your sweetness,
for the daylight searches too deep
    into my cherished dreams,
 and the noon sun is too bright
     to read the echoes
that haunt my midnight sleep.

THE GIRL

The girl sat alone, at rest in the summer sun,
her hair like molten fire, red, burnished
where shadows of weeping willow
cast long thin fingers across her form.
She was at peace, one with the slow moving
river as it softly fought its way between
the heavy fern lined banks of high season.
She was one with the shadows, a deeper form
and so still she could have been imagination,
a ghost from another time long since gone.
Yet her shirt was short and the length of her
legs brown with other days spent in the sun.
Her eyes looked off to the far distant hills
past the running river hung with reed and beech,
unaware of the soft scolding of blackbirds
that so loudly objected to her presence there.
She would not have cared anyway, the red
haired girl, nor would she care that she was
alone, seemingly friendless there,
for she was part of the earth around her
at one with the sun and grass and air.
She neither knew or heeded the approving
eyes of others as they hurried past her silent place.
So she sat, her pretty face and youth
untarnished for she needed nothing beyond
what she already had found by the river.
For here was peace, such tranquil peace that it
spoke of heaven and angels and some deep
fulfilment beyond her youthful years or age.

SOMNOLENT CRESCENT MOON

The moon hung golden against the backdrop of a starry sky, somnolent, hazy, casting shadows onto dew kissed grass, and in her light, tinged golden against darker trees, a fox moved swiftly, casting round for the scent of night wandering rabbits, whiskers etched white by moonlight against the burgundy of his coat.

And still the moon hung, rising, heavier now, shrouded in mist curling cross summer filled fields of barley and yellow wheat where tiny animals rustled and took their fill of abundance, wary of barn owls sweeping silently through the dark, eyes wide and yellow, seeing every blade of grass stark and sharp against the white light of the moon.

Coming dawn and the moon washed by morning cloud, glazed with a deeper gold shone on the hushed movements of a man, as stealthily he crept through the woods, working the trail, oblivious of the life that shuddered and hid at the sound of his silent feet, terrified by his great height and smell and form against the black of the deeper night.

Somnolent crescent moon hanging pale, ghostly just before sunrise, gilded white by bursting rising sunshine, melting softly away with the silence of night and the shadowy mystery of a world unseen except by fox and owl and badger, unknown to any man other than the silent poacher, his coat damp with mud, boots dark against the green of summer meadow.

A June Storm

Sitting hushed in silent rain,
windows smeared with tears,
rain caught in blown wet roses.
Lightning briefly sparks and cracks,
fizzing behind shadowed hills.
Rolling thunder, dark swollen clouds,
stretching dark fingers to
torment bending twisting trees.

Silent deep shadows, hushed rain
dripping sullen, darkly into heavy
shrouded gardens, caught by
shimmering lilac and mighty oak.
Darker sky, sketched with grey,
seared red, though darkened noon.

A last howl of mighty wind,
silent throbbing shadows dying,
fading cloud blown skies, shrouded
mist hidden day, muffled and still.
Bright sun briefly casts its smile
across rain soaked fields, battered
ruined harvest, and softly blowing trees.

THE HAUNTED WOOD

Here, in the woods, the easterly wind blows,
catching and sighing in the high boughs
of leafy green.
Yet, except for that soft whisper, there is silence
as dusk reaches her fingers further into the
deeper shadows.
A pond lies, heavily shrouded with evening mist,
deep and dark, the holder of secrets
and fear.
An owl waits, softly, softly, ready to kill,
as the full moon begins her ascent into
the night sky.
And in the deeper hidden depth of the woods
the ghosts of past mortals walk forever lost
in fallen misery.
No man, nor beast, walk that haunted wood,
where things lurk that should not be
and shadows cry.
So time passes, and the haunted forest slumbers,
waiting to catch the unwary traveller,
always waiting.

GOD

Can we seek God, our Lord, by prayer and supplication,
or by listening to the mumbling of our ancient truth?
Can the Church, made of finite man and sin,
be truly able to illuminate the face of heaven?

Throughout History, man has sought the truth of religion,
cloaked in hypocrisy, tapestry and lies,
for has not man, killed and plundered hidden lands
with the Bible tucked beneath his arm?

And having dragged heathen men to our beliefs,
we leave them naked, confused, alone,
while we return to the lands of our Christianity,
smug in the rapture to come.

Yet God, if He sent His son to die upon the cross,
surely never looked to see how man would
use His words as weapons, pouring hatred and fear
into a new, more dangerous world?

'Armageddon' looms, dark in the shadow of its coming,
while we scream loudly to the Lord on high,
'is He dead' or a concept of our minds like any little
god to boost our need for fulfilment?

And if He is real, He is far away from the puny lives of man,
waiting for us to realise the pain of our own wanting,
lost in the ghettos of prejudice, avarice and pride
waiting for Him to reveal the truth before we die.

The world is an old, washed-out place, waiting for the end to come,
and man is confused, his awareness dimmed by time.
Religion cannot be justified by the passing of history
nor regarded as nothing more than an illusion.

Man is God himself, mortal ordained priests of rapture,
offering religion to the empty minds of humanity,
knowing that we are near the end of time, empty and lost,
waiting for the annihilation that must come to us all.

WORDS ARE JUST

Words are but soundless noise
unless they are spoken with love
and arms that hold are empty
if they do not hold with passion.
Eyes are blinded to beauty
unless the soul is reborn
to light and tender touch.
Truth is nothing but shadows
unless the speaker believes them
and love is a mere thought
until it is spoken aloud.
Truth lies within each person,
as does love and passion,
if only the essence of life
can be released into the light.

Dawn

Dawn, and silently the morning breeze
billowed the lace curtains,
white ghosts, delicate gossamer
in the grayness of light
spilling across the bedroom floor.
Stirring, I listened to hear only
silence, the bliss of harmony of
peaceful sleeping children,
and for a moment my heart was
full and warm for their life and mine.
Gently, sweetly far off chimes tinkled,
laughing as the growing wind
pushed morning birdsong
against the glory of the rising sun,
and again I knew the sheer joy
of a summer day, waiting fresh
and untouched just for me
as delicate and hopeful
as I wished it to be.

SUNSET AT SEA

The sea against sunset sky
lay like a charcoal drawing,
soft lines, blurred edges, smudged
shapes of dark rock against
black cliffs,
and behind soft gray clouds
fading in hue, then blazing again
to the colours of a Turner painting,
muted rose, pink and golden yellow.
In the distance lingered
long distant ships, silhouetted on
the horizon by dying sun shadows.
Hesitantly a breath of wind sighed
against shallow silver waves
where they rushed on the incoming
tide to the darkened beach.
In the distance a dog barked
answered by a hunting fox.
Softly, tinged lingeringly with rose
the dying sun shivered and
sank behind the night cloud.

Today

Yesterday I was a child, and tomorrow I will be old,
but today I held children to my breast, took lovers
to my bed, was fearful and at the same time brave.
I loved and was loved, judged, took pity and was pitied,
felt travail and pain, and sheer unadulterated joy.
I felt the wind in my hair and the touch of wind on
my skin, knew life and sorrowed at death.
I learnt to be a woman, but never forgot what it was
like to be a child, I listened and was listened to.
I travelled the world and stayed at home, I looked
into the soul of others and bared my own soul to friends.
I learnt to give, but was never ashamed to take,
to share my wealth and never bewail my poverty.
I struggled to make ends meet, but gloried in the joy
of motherhood, watching babies grow to men,
take wives and produce babies of their own.
I have worked hard and played hard, invigorated by
health and the means to live my life as I wished.
I have walked miles of heath and hill and let the peace
of nature rest in my soul, picked bluebells and
danced with flowers in my hair and joy in my heart.
Yesterday I knew nothing of life, and tomorrow I will
have no memory of youth, but today I have life,
and hope in my heart and freedom and peace.

STAN MCKERRON

Stan is married to Wilma; they live in Aberdeen. They have a daughter, Fiona, who lives in Johannesburg with her husband, Carl, and son, Matthew. Their son, Jim, lives in Altrincham. They all support Manchester United.

Stan has worked in engineering for all of his adult life, and he has been a Commercial Publications Manager for the past twenty years.

He wrote *Circle Of Life* several years ago after completing a Creative Writing Course.

His hobbies include writing, reading, collecting and creating board games.

CIRCLE OF LIFE

Crying, ill at ease.
His needs paramount, his wants manifest.
His flesh sticky, slimy, wet, cold; craving dry, touching warmth.
His giving, bending bones aching from the long, slow, forced deliverance into a new space.
His worldly consciousness a long-lost mystery.
Alone, crying for friendly favours.

Lying, ill-formed.
In conflict, remembering a life to come.
Reflecting on what could have been, must be.
Forgetful by immaculate design; a soul in ever-darkening shadow, a body bursting with raw, material growth.
Letting go as needs must, but sad - so sad for losing truth, to gain mere independence.
Remembering deep, tingling, warm feelings; the brilliant, white, yellow, orange and gold light, the belonging, the love.
Relearning a separate life; clinging for consolation, a pathetic panacea.
Hoping for maternal comfort, for inner strength, for a life-time's resolve.
A soul fast fading.

Crawling, on the make.
His earth-bound consciousness in manufacture, happenstance looking back at his future; now glimpsing the light through ten thousand hours of separating shadows.
Touching with grubby, fleshy hands, tasting the fruits of hard labour; slipping and sliding headlong into the abyss.
Hesitating, now catching furtive glints of truth through a veiled mist; then content in his ignorance; unsure.
Constantly side-tracked by a sophisticated, substantial, diabolic reality.
Hearing familiar, vicarious voices; sometimes soft, warm, subtle; sometimes sharp, shattering, severe; but ever welcome.
Desperate to belong at any cost.
A soul seeking solace.

Staggering, drunk before his time.
Stronger of arm with each passing day; trying, testing, tampering, a naughty neophyte.
Remembering still a distant place, a now foreign feeling, a forgotten freedom; receiving random sparks of spurious space-time.
A soul obscured by a myriad layers, a labyrinth of esoteric emotion, waiting to strike with vituperative vehemence.
Watching, acting, reacting; subtracting perfection, adding imperfection, carelessly.
Chasing his destiny with rapacious relish.
Drifting apart, yet becoming a part; knowing not the paths of truth, nor suspecting the dangers of naiveté.
An apprentice homo sapien, learning his craft from shoddy workmen.
A soul submerged.

Walking, searching for the world.
Detached in the midst of the throng; purposefully,
inevitably isolated from the perfect, pure light.
Suffering, as young men do for the sins of their
fathers.
Watching others constructing walls; retaliating;
erecting empirical fences, marking out tentative
boundaries, successfully.
Yet, frantically building bridges, fearfully filling
the gap; wanting courage to stand alone.
Consciously communicating with self, with others;
reading, writing, speaking; performing a part with
increasing, calculating confidence.
A man in the making, a man of this world.
At times happy, not knowing; at times sad, not knowing
driven by a worldly, slipshod, unholy,
contemporary instinct.
A part of something inferred, never spoken, never
described; languishing within a facile framework;
feeling fragile, frustrated; now flippant, then
foolish; now foreign, friendless, then festive,
fellow-feeling.
All things to all men, outside; tormented within.
Gullible, guilty, gangling, gauche; yet gifted, gentle, genial.
Taking, not giving.
*A God-given body, sculpted from star-dust; a consciousness
cobbled casually.*

Skipping, well-disposed.
His yesterdays served, thinking only of today, tomorrow.
His soul a cosmic conundrum; a light-gaoler; a closet of ethereal essence, part filled with hidden heartache, heartfelt hurt.
Questioning, not accepting; now a country member, a player, a taxpayer, a self-styled proselyte.
Understanding the rules, having measured each length laboriously each breadth blandly, each height heedfully; a time-served technicist; an unforgiving, under-evolved, rag-tag radical.
A temerarious terror, a terrigenous taker, a tactless taxonomist; an unholy triumvirate.
Off the leash, enjoying; enthusiastically experimenting; ecstatically exploring; elatedly examining; exalted by an earned emancipation.
Making decisions for self; keeping one ear for Daddy's didacticism, Mummy's moralising; yet, hard of hearing.
A body built - nowhere to grow; now complete, life-size, adult, amen.
Standing at the summit, seeing all; nothing hidden, nothing forbidden; no thought for the journey ahead - not noticing the imperceptible downward slope.
A consciousness on auto-pilot.

Striding, taking no prisoners.
A soul somewhere, not sought.
Controlling, confident; caught up in the crowd; cheerfully
chiding, charmingly cajoling; charismatic.
A man of his time, with time; nesciently, nicely doing time.
A family man; producing, providing; part of a pack of
his own propagation; proud, pleased, privileged.
Giving, having received, not untenable, promised, soft
things - but real, material, hard things; possessing
now prepared to pay.
Making and achieving goals; a goalkeeper.
Driven by a shallow, spartan, slip-streamed consciousness;
glossing over life's little doubts; manufacturing
malevolent, motionless mind-mire.
In his head, living and sharing the good life; selfish
only by default; not intending to let his nearest be
farthest, his most be least; gathering rocks.
Worldly-wise; an earthling.

Ambling, uncertain.
Of two minds; one by necessity tuned to terra firma, the
other fluctuating around a firmamental frequency.
Handling with small heart the humdrum; reaping reasonable
reward for routine responsibilities.
Treading water; not passively, but actively serving a
second apprenticeship; practising an ancient
alchemical craft; realigning, readjusting; just forty
footsteps along a wearisome, winding road; happily
heading home.
Searching, researching; looking for truth.
Knowing more, yet understanding less; a victim of his
own decisions, a product of his own imagination.
Questioning the fundamentals of life; not accepting the
accepted view; at odds with his very being; pursuing an
impalpable paradox.
Conscious of his consciousness; believing the unbelievable;
realising the riddle of reality.
Seeking a spent soul; hoping to rekindle the fabulous
fire; to make contact; to bathe in the glorious,
golden, God-given glow.
A *maybe mortal, middlemost mind-manipulator.*

Shuffling, in no hurry.
Forty times forty footsteps closer to the loving, living light; a myriad spiritual, spiral stairways to climb.
Unflinching, dedicated, determined; perpetrating an inside job.
Restoring a suppressed, subliminal, sublime soul; carefully peeling away the calluses formed by former fearful feelings.
Touching what the hand cannot feel; seeing with another eye The Architects' glorious creation; sensing all with a madness scorned by a blind, blinkered, bland establishment.
Living for today, now; neither looking backwards nor forwards; resisting the charming futility; giving vitality to the tenuous reality of the moment.
Reasoning; no longer submitting to his conscious's serpentine soliloquies, rather reacting with a rational, rectitudinal response.
A man, a craftsman with a mission; closing the chasm, stitching together that which was torn asunder by a lifetime's lachrymose lolloping.

Dying, at peace with his old space.
Living within; without the hoi polloi; separate, but not alone.
Not communicating on an earthly frequency; at times confabulating with his cosmic cohorts via a once redundant, reformed route; sometimes in conversation with self-reviewing, restating, regurgitating; remembering earthly, existential experiences.
Expecting an elemental ending; elated, yet seduced by a seditious sentimentality.
Waiting to swap spaces, places.

Flying, homeward-bound.
Hovering above his old space; looking back at the empty, mortal remains of his former self; a spirit lighter than air, momentarily weighed down by earth-bound evocations.
Now flying fast, fearlessly, forever forward.
Feeling the burdens of a life slip away; seeing, with everlasting eyes the confined, comfortable conduit spiralling towards a beckoning, bright beacon.
Not touching, not concerned.
Falling, though not afraid.
Conscious of being; relieved, expectant; tearing through a tranquil tube, weightless, watching.
Perceiving a growing, golden glow; a distant, divine destiny.
Recognising a fast-approaching, familiar form; wanting for words; tingling, giving, loving.
Home, hallelujah, amen.

Yvonne Marie Beattie

My name is Yvonne Marie Beattie.

I was born on the 24th January 1962 and I was brought up in the little village of Renton in Dunbartonshire, Scotland. I am the second eldest of five children and was raised in the Roman Catholic faith by my parents William Beattie and Sylvia (Gilfeather) Beattie. Despite suffering from albinism from birth and being registered partially sighted I still managed to go through mainstream schooling. I attended St Martin's Primary in Renton before transferring to Notre Dame High in Dumbarton, where my flair for poetry was first noticed. I finally left school in 1978.

After leaving school I did various types of work. My first job was in an old peoples' home as a care assistant before moving on to a job as a catering assistant in a local hospital. I also worked as a housemaid in a local hotel. I moved out of the area to start a job as a live-in housemaid in The Royal Hotel in Dunkeld, Perthshire. This is where I met my now ex-husband Aidan and where we were married. We had three children. Bryan, Andrew and Coleen. Shortly after the birth of my first son we returned back to the Renton area and we have lived in the surrounding area ever since. The main reasons I write poetry is to help me express my feelings more clearly and also because I find it therapeutic and very enjoyable too. The main influences and inspiration for my poetry are mostly taken from true life events that have touched my own personal life. These include the brutal murder of my older brother Richard Beattie aged 32 years and the death of my younger brother David from cancer aged 31 years and the ongoing feelings of loss, pain, anger, heartache and so on.

I have various interests which include spending time with my three teenage children, creative writing, listening to a variety of different types of music, walking and spending time with my family and friends.

I would like to say thank you to everyone who has supported and encouraged me with my poetry writing.

FEELINGS

My feelings so often mixed up
Tinged with confusion and sadness too,
So unsure of myself,
And where my life was leading to.

The inner need to find myself,
The person I thought completely lost,
To rediscover the real me -
No matter what the cost.

You came along and seemed to know,
The turmoil I was going through.
In the midst of all my sadness,
Our special friendship grew.

So many times you picked me up
When I was feeling really low
With a smile or a phone call
Or the words of encouragement you would show.

You are a special person
Who was there to help me through,
But before too long I realised
I should break contact with you.

Being honest deep down it was the last thing I wanted to do,
So the final decision I have to give to you,
As you may find it easier to do.
If that's the way it has to be, then there's nothing I can do.

I would like a final chance to say goodbye, wish you all the best,
To say a special thank you for being there for me.
I know you realise the happiness and feelings I found with you,
A special reminder for me to hold on to.

A Plea For Justice

I am writing my plea
In memory of someone so dear.
Loved but lost within the last year.
So brutally and tragically killed on Tuesday 4th of May.

Gone but not forgotten at the end of each day.
I ask everyone out there to sit back and think
If a piece of information known is a vital link.
Could they hold the answers to many questions to date?
Only hoping these answers won't come too late

To bring justice at last for the life taken away
From dear Richard (Dick) Beattie on that 4th day in May
To his friends and his family who all bear the cost
Of a dear son, husband, brother, grandson, uncle, nephew, cousin,
and friend now lost.

I have spoken out now maybe I should have from the start:
At times it's hard to put into words what you feel in your heart.
I will draw to a close as there's not much more I can say
Except if you have any information please don't hide it away.

Springtime

Springtime is my favourite time of year,
The dark nights gradually becoming clear,
The signs of new life all around,
Flowers now shooting through the cold and solid ground.

Nature still has so many wonders to unfold,
So much beauty for my eyes to behold.
The snowdrops and crocuses are now in full bloom,
Without even the slightest hint of perfume.

The birds are so busy building their nests,
The young calves and lambs in fields of green.
A clear blue sky the sun breaking through.
Adds the final touch to a perfect view.

I love to go walking on a fresh spring day.
It helps me unwind and to chase my worries away.
So many happy, smiling people that I may meet,
Which can only help to make a perfect day totally complete.

THE TUNNEL OF DESPAIR

Trapped inside this black tunnel
Shadows of despair so close behind
Strong memories of loss and rejection.

The feeling that there is no way forward,
Just no reason to get out of bed.
The overwhelming thought and dread,
Constantly wishing I was dead.

The days seem to last forever,
I am no longer in control.
Drained of strength and so very low,
No more energy no get up and go.

My nerves are now at breaking point,
Stomach so churned up inside.
Can't bear to think of food or eating,
These facts I try hard to hide.

Not the slightest glint of hope remaining,
No tiny flicker of light.
No one left now to turn to,
All alone to try and make it through.

THE OVERWHELMING SHADOWS

The overwhelming shadows in the corners of my mind
Sometimes bring such sadness, peace and rest are hard to find.
So many questions left unanswered, doubts and inner fears
The hardest part of all is accepting you're no longer here.

My thoughts return to that sunny morning Tuesday 4th of May,
All the sadness which unfolded before the end of day.
I had still to learn your life was so brutally taken away,
And come to bear this sadness which is here to stay.

My memories I treasure because they can't be taken away.
They are precious and they're mine on a sad and lonely day.
Some are happy, some are sad, some are the best we ever had.
They make me feel so thankful and so very glad.

This nightmare started over two years ago.
When will it end, I really don't know.
I will carry on pretending, put on a brave smile.
Just make believe everything is fine for a while.
I have got to be strong, it's expected you see.
Hide all these feelings deep inside me.

Now I want to make a fresh start.
Follow these feelings deep down in my heart.
Pick up the pieces, carry on with my fight.
For truth, justice and all that is right.

ASPECTS OF LOVE

Love's a very precious gift
Which can bestow such happiness and joy
Like a perfect vision of a clear blue sky,
An added warmth from the sunshine's shimmering glow,
Shining for us to see here below.

But once in a while love can twist and change route
Turning our emotions upside down.
The anger, sadness, sorrow, pain, and lastly saying goodbye
Just like an angry, dark clouded sky,
Raindrops the tears that fall from on high.

The hardest lesson of love:
To watch a loved one fade away,
Suffering so much pain without complaint.
I would have given anything just to see your pain cease
And your strength to return and increase.

Instead I got prepared for the final outcome lingering in my mind
Put my selfish feelings to keep you here far behind
Accept that I had to let you go, which was so hard to do.
You were not only my caring, loving brother Dave
But a special friend too.

My memories I will treasure
In a special place inside my heart.
This love will keep you near me Dave, not so far apart,
When I watch the free birds flying in the sky above,
A sign that you are now pain free and surrounded by heavenly love.

Anger

My anger such a negative force
So powerful and destructive too
Which does emerge every now and then,
Bringing those inner fears and shadows back into full view

Like a volcano welling up inside,
Its carnage just waiting to reap,
An inner struggle to gain control,
Until this anger subsides and is once more beat.

Is this anger so deep rooted.
Brought about by the actions of someone else?
Yes at times this could be so.
But being honest I am much more angry with myself.

When all the ghosts and hurts of the past,
The lessons learned now shining clear,
Don't let anyone get too near
As the price to pay could be so costly I fear.

So build that wall so high and strong
Making sure that no one can get near,
Never to see my vulnerable and caring side
Because it is safely locked inside.

So nothing can hurt or harm me now.
I know my anger is negative.
What other people may fail to see:
It is also a coat of armour that can protect me.

Just For You

I felt so sad when I found out
You could be leaving soon.
I guess some day it had to be.
Because it seems so clear now,
You feel so differently from me.

Being honest I realised sometime ago
Just how deep my feelings went.
But rather than risking losing you,
I tried to settle just for friends.

So many sad and mixed up feelings
Would emerge every now and then.
So long as you were there,
Remained the hope that you did care.

Now your future plans seem made.
No more choices now but to let go.
Were you scared of being hurt?
As I know the pain that this can bring.

Just unable to completely trust me.
All those feelings I tried to show,
Which came straight from my heart.
That is something you should know.

THE SWIFT THIEF

The winds of change that confine me
Came swirling around so fast,
Without the slightest prior warning,
Everything now so dark and overcast.

The thief that came to visit,
Ducking and diving in the night,
To watch over his potential prey,
Poised and waiting to strike.

His swag bag held tight in his hand
To conceal all that he planned to swipe,
Filling his bag to the brim,
With not a thought for me in sight.

He turns to make his getaway,
Leaving me so far behind,
All my love, hopes, and dreams,
Lying torn, tattered, and tossed aside.

So beware of the thief who calls in the night,
As he will vanish without a trace,
Leaving feelings of sadness and rejection,
finally and firmly in his place.

ALWAYS FRIENDS

Thinking back to when we first met
We really could never have known
How special our friendship would become.
Through the years how it has grown.

From day to day and year by year
How much we helped each other through
Not only in the happy times.
But sharing the bad times too.

Through the laughter and the tears
It was always nice to know
That you would be there,
My own special friend who always cared.

Now you have to move on,
To make a new and fresh start.
I wish you happiness and good luck
From the bottom of my heart.
You will always be close in my thoughts.

MY LITTLE TREASURE

I have a tiny little treasure
I hold so close within my heart.
It always helps me through
When things seem really hard.

It stirs deep in my heart
Gives me the courage to carry on.
This little bit of hope
Reassures me and helps me to be strong.

It keeps me pushing on
Sometimes slowly day by day.
This little light of hope
Will guide me on my way.

I will hold on to this precious gift
Keep it safely tucked away
To grow steadily if I can,
My little bit of magic always close at hand.

As these hopes grow stronger
I know one day I will find
An inner peace and contentment,
Love and happiness in time.

A Lament For Them All

For all the forgotten victims,
For every murder case that remains unsolved,
Their families' nightmare still lives on,
The brutal murder of their loved one never gone.

The overwhelming loss, heartache, pain, every day they go through
Even though they have now been laid to rest.
After such a long and painful time,
Old news so easily forgotten,
But not for the victims' families left behind.

The awful trauma still replays each and every day,
Constantly over and over in their minds.
The endless days the sleepless nights,
Overwhelming feelings of despair and sadness too.

The law system that should protect them
Has failed the victims and their families too.
No perpetrators brought to answer
For the barbaric crimes they do.

The case remains unsolved but open.
No more publicity can be sought,
No hope of it being rehighlighted,
The chance of new evidence are rated as not a lot.

So then emerges the forgotten families
Which other people may find hard to completely comprehend.
Outsiders may feel you should let it be.
My answer would have to be I pray this on going trauma
Is something I would never want anyone else to see.

TERRY IRELAND

I was born in the East Yorkshire village of Withernwick, between Hull and Hornsea. My childhood was rich in everything but money and possessions. My greatest friends are from the village, many of us still keep in touch, though scattered now.

I joined the regular army at eighteen and spent more than two years in Germany making friends in a small village. This period influenced me almost as much as my own village life. The values seemed almost identical.

I had various jobs before spending twenty years at the Prudential, taking early retirement at fifty, and losing all my money in a business venture. I now work as a canvasser for a double glazing company. I've been married for thirty years with two grown children.

I remember as a teenager enjoying so much the work of T S Elliott but being very angry at the amount of reference books and classical knowledge needed to appreciate him fully. I have been writing since childhood, and decided I needed to write for people like myself, who wanted something easily understood but not condescending. Poetry should be for everybody, not a small elite, and deal with life. This has been one of my main motivations.

I love country music and the depth and simplicity of emotions it expresses. this has also been a great influence for more than forty years.

I write about anything that excites or interests me, latterly a lot of autobiographical work and humorous poetry. I am a lifelong socialist horrified at the transformation in our society wrought by Thatcherism, and perpetuated by new labour. This also tends to influence my work.

I have led a very happy life. I am glad I was born when I was, rather than in the current society. I hope my work reflects this general contentment.

SHOES

stranger
shoes clean and shiny and neat
sensibly encasing two small feet

    friend
    shoes keeping step two pairs
    walking paths climbing stairs

        lover
        shoes side by side properly standing
        clothes neatly folded on the landing

            stranger
            shoes one knocked over askew by its pair
            angrily she dresses to run down the stair

                end
                shoe heels clack hard down concrete
                across the path and along the street

                    stranger
                      friend
                        lover
                          stranger
                              end.

Sunday Morning, Post Waltzing Weasel

the life and soul of last night's party
views with dread
the very thought
of moving his head
well aware of the daggery pain
that would stab and scour
each corner of his brain
leaving him exhausted.

fragments of remembrances of conversations
drift slowly through his mind
making him seem fascist
uncaring and unkind

the breakfast he ate for bravado
bacon and eggs warm and greasy
lie on a stomach
already queasy
making him vow
never again
if I survive
if I escape
this hangover alive

NOVEMBER 1993

we meet on those weeks
that we sign on the dole
nod but don't speak
each learning his role
redundant unused.

does he feel like me
barely hiding the hate
at friends' comments
about living on the state
through they're only a joke.

I tell them about us
two ordinary blokes
each fortnight at three
waiting to hear
the call of his name
each starting to fear
he is to blame

We both used to stride
tall through the door
now we seem to slide
from holes in the floor.
do my eyes drift away
from meeting others' gaze
do my shoulders slump
and I still in that phase.

What we used to be
doesn't matter any more
please silently leave
closing the door

WITHERNWICK, NOW

in the village where I was born
there was always lots of trees
especially those in the churchyard
that gently swayed in the breeze
I suppose there must have been storms
when those branches swung and thrashed
and there must have been times
when branches split and smashed
but overhanging our cottage
those giants to my child's eyes
sent me to sleep
with their whispers and sighs.
and woke me in the morning
as they played along
to the chorus
of dawn bird song.
some carry my name
carved with my first knife
all boys had one then
part of country life.

I sheltered from rain under those trees
trunks tightly gripped between my knees
as tightly as I would later hold any lover
as I scrambled as high as I dared to look over
the village the world my world spread below

Most of those trees like my family
are now dead and gone
those that are left shelter the graves
for us survivors who've moved on.
I rarely go back now
I feel so alone
but I keep the village in my memories
and the village keeps the bones.

Post Cod War Blues, November 1991

St Andrews fish dock has been closed down
      for there's barely a fleet to sail from the town
      the old lock gates where the trawlers queued
      to land for the markets are no longer used
      a metalled road runs over the lock
      and no water runs between river and dock
      buildings are tumbled or razed to the ground
      and it's quiet and eerie with only the sounds
      of the water and wind and shrieks of the gulls
      this Sunday morning in the old docks of Hull
      it's forlorn and deserted and so cold and bleak
      I'll cuddle the fire for the rest of the week
      but I need to watch it as it finally goes
      I need to remember so my kids will know
they've filled one dock in with mud and sand
      there's probably a subsidy for reclaiming land
      and thrown up warehouses and the usual shops
      to erase our past so one history stops
      there's a bowling alley to practice ten-pin
      and as much fast food as you can cram in
      this is the future and it's brash and it's bold
      this is the era of grab all you can hold.
      it's taken my city and torn out its soul
      for there's no pride in claiming the dole
they say this is progress and progress is all
      so bugger the memories of those on the Gaul
      and bugger the hardships and bugger the pain
      and bugger the families who'll never see again
      the pride and the swagger of the trawler wage earner
      or the newly wise eyes of the young deckie learner
      there's no more last beer and fast taxi rides
      to jump from the lock as she sails with the tide

now it's heaven bless the poor and heaven bless the sick
    and heaven bless the slow and heaven bless the thick
    and heaven bless those with their backs to the wall
    whilst for the few winners it's bugger you all

GIRL

platform 9,
Hull Paragon station,
1959

    I used to see her every day
    I knew she was nice
    in the nicest of ways.
    Not too tall not too slim
    dressed for work
    smart and trim.
    She would smile I would nod
    but neither spoke
    the unspoken rule neither broke.
    Every day I checked her hands
    for engagement ring
    or wedding band.
I knew we'd meet when the time was right
laugh with our friends at our morning rite
    Then one day she wasn't there.
    I didn't know why didn't care.
    I only knew it hurt a lot
    and though time healed
    I never forgot.

Derbyshire

The voice of Hank Williams slides round the room
Singing his words of love and despair
Calling to me across forty odd years
I've lived some, I've seen some I've been there.

The evening meal rests on my belly
As I sit and look at dear friends
Almost supine along the settee
A not quite pair of bookends.

There's a feeling of warmth in this house
That doesn't just come from the fire
It comes from their feelings of love and trust
Their air of fulfilled desire.

For every woman a husband and lover
To every man a mistress and wife
For the fortunate few
All four roles are played by just two
For a happy and simplified life.

Pigeons

I am one of the pigeons that live on Wilberforce's head
which in pigeon meritocracy puts me near the top
between those on the city and guildhalls
and those on the better type of shop.

I got this position by birthright
we've been here since 19 and 10
inspite of attempts to remove us
every now and then

when somebody in power
seemed to get an urge
and bang before we knew it
it's on with another purge.

so mr city councillor if in passing
I leave a message on your hat
just regard it as a greeting
from an avian aristocrat

CREATION

wasn't God clever
he made the end of the land
where the waters began
with the odd stretches of sand
where the waters expand
and the cliffs all and neat
to save getting wet feet
and just to make sure the tide
doesn't rise too soon
he put the controls
up there on the moon
       not so
       very near
       for us to touch
       or interfere
       so it still works
       after all these years

SMALL STEPS

three steps forward
two steps back
a meandering type of progress
along life's track.
quick steps slow steps
they all add up the same
a relentless rate of progress
through life's game
it doesn't really matter
what steps you take
and it doesn't really matter
what route you take
marching straight forward
or taking the odd bend
they all add up to small steps
nearer to the end.

FINGERS

fingers
    trace paths
    down bodies
    for mouths
    and tongues
    to follow
gently
    they lie entwined
    three sets of lips
    working
    in the double kiss
    of love

Ann Grimwood

I am thirty-two years of age and have always had an interest in poetry. I was brought up by the local authority and in times when I felt I had no one to talk to, I used to write poetry about my experiences and how I was feeling. I found it very therapeutic. I really began to write seriously about five years ago when my foster dad died. There were so many issues going on around me, and I found that people were very wary of showing their true feelings and would never talk about issues around them. Issues like war, homelessness, depression, bereavement, and I wanted to show people that it is alright to talk about their problems and that they are not alone. I feel that I have gone some way to achieving my goal. I have had 161 poems published in various poetry magazines and anthologies and I feel that my voice is now being heard. Poetry is my life now, it has become more than a hobby. Apart from my children, it is the thing that is closest to my heart.

Ann's Poem

You wanted a china doll, they gave you a baby
You broke the china doll, she was too fragile for you
You dropped her on the concrete floor
And broke her head in two
The china doll cracked, and the baby cried
Daddy gave the doll away to someone who could mend her
Your baby girl was here to stay, with nowhere you could send her
But in your mind the doll had died
And in her cot the baby cried
You couldn't recognise the pain from emptiness inside
The china doll is mended, another child can hold her
Your baby grew - away from you
You were afraid to touch her in case you spoiled her
Maybe you broke her
Now that childhood's ended, and you want her friendship
And think a smile will do, to mend the fragile crack that grew
Inside her mind when love was scarce, and life was too unkind
A china doll can feel no pain, its painted face is smiling
But in your daughter's grown up mind
there is still a baby crying.

I'll Share Your Burden

Don't feel so lost, Don't retreat into a shell
A time will come when everything will turn out well
You may feel now that you're not worthy of anybody's love
But have faith in the Lord above
You may think people don't care
But believe me the Lord will always be there
He'll help you through your suffering
He will share your pain
Maybe when you feel His love for you
You'll feel safe again.

MIRROR MIRROR

Look in the mirror and you will see the inner being hiding within you
The secret part of your soul that you sometimes find so hard to show
An inner part of you that you don't want people to know
For you can pretend to yourself for that is OK
But when dealing with others, our insecurities we lock away
For it is easier to put up barriers than to find yourself getting used
For they can attack your physical body
But your soul they will never be able to bruise
For this is the part of you that has built up many walls
That has ignored others, when they have called
the insensitive part of you that may have laid dormant for years
A place built up by your childhood fears
But the mirror never lies, and you will find this to be true
For it can see the part of you, that you are trying so hard to lose.

A BURNING

Shouting, screaming they drag her to the pyre
Uncommitted crimes consigned to punishing fire
She struggles to free bound hands and limbs
As the crowd hurl stones and justice light dims
Before flaming branches spotlight the pitiful wretch
Hysterical glee incites the bloodlust crowd to fetch
More brands: she curses them as the flames soar higher
Leaving charred remains
A finger pointing to the sky
Another so-called witch, tried by fools of sick mirth
Her only crime, for helping the sick
And being at one with the earth.

It's My Decision

It's my decision, it's my choice what to do
So why make me feel that I owe so much to you
You're not willing to listen
To anything I do or say
Why don't you just leave me alone
Or just go away
Each day you ask me what you think I should do
I think you already know the answer, because I certainly do
I can't kill something that has the right to be born
I can't play around with another's life even though I feel so forlorn
I know you won't stay around to see your daughter or your son
But I'm telling you now, I'm not giving up the chance of being a mum
For years my life has been full of pain
I'm not going to go through that situation again and again
So if you decide to leave me, and make me go it alone
Don't expect to see your child, don't even try to phone
You had your chance you blew it, it showed you didn't care
So don't come crawling back to me, because I no longer want you here
And when your child is older and asks about her dad
I'll just tell her you didn't want her, and from the beginning you
                                                                never had
But she won't go without love from me
And she'll never feel alone
And at least with me she will have a parent, and a happy home.

Don't Worry

Hey little girl wipe away your tears
Let me help you confront your past fears
Open up and ell me what went wrong
Come on you can trust me, here you will always belong
Let me share the pain that for years has haunted you
Let me help you see the bad times through
I'm here to listen, I do care
When you pass our doorstep, please leave your problems there
It's not your fault what happened, you weren't old enough to
                                                    understand.
Your fate was then determined by a callous man
He abused you and took away your self worth
Come on cry the tears that you have held back
Start to believe that there is somewhere you can go
Remember the good times instead of the bad
And forget the memories of your step-dad
Look forward to the future and all the good things to come
For I'm here to help you
And you no longer have to feel so empty and numb.

To Let You Know

When you see the leaves moving silently in the breeze
Think not of the weather, instead think of me
With each wave that crashes against the shore
Let it remind you that I am here for ever more
Let each raindrop be my tears, let them caress your face
Let it be known then that I have gone to a better place
And as the sun breaks slowly through the trees
Do not be afraid for it is only me.

By Royal Appointment

Each day their life is planned for them
Places to go people to see
They don't get a day off, from their appointments they are never free
The Queen attends functions gives her name to good causes
While Princess Anne is happy when attending to her horses
Charles does his bit for the homeless
He is happy when helping others
Fergie and Diana are just happy being mothers
Such a big family, with so much to do
Still have time to help people see the bad times through
Giving so much of themselves, not having time to be alone
It's not an easy life when you are appointed to the throne.

The Morning After

Too tired to move, my head feels like lead
Friends have gone, was it something I said
Did I make a fool of myself last night?
Was I again trying to pick a fight?
I force myself to move but my brain seems to have shut down
The price I pay for one night on the town
My tongue now resembles the carpet
My breath smells like something the dog dragged in
The only reminder that it happened is the overflowing bin
I tell myself never again, I won't touch another drink
I've said it all before though, two days the hangover will be gone
Then it will be back to the pub I think.

My Precious Baby

Seeing you lying there, makes my heart skip a beat
You're so very perfect, right down to your tiny feet
The way you look at me when I talk to you
Makes me feel so good inside
My darling Carrie Ann, my love for you I cannot hide
I'm not treating you as a replacement for the children I've lost
Because you're your own person, and usually let me know who's boss
I will never harm you, or send you away
Because Mummy loves you, and that love's here to stay
I hope when you're older that our bond stays as strong
I hope if you have any problems, that you will be able to turn to me
Because I want you to know, Mum will always be around.

I'm No Different

Look at me when you speak
Stop turning the other way
I'm no different from you
no matter what others might say
People always condemn me
For the things I say or do
I'm not a freak, I have feelings too
I have love to give, I have a lot of time to share
Is it too much to ask to want somebody to care
Having Down Syndrome would not mean I would love you any less
Please just give me a chance
I will do the rest.

CHILD ABUSE - THE CHILD'S STORY

The boy huddles in the corner surrounded by pain
He thought he loved him, he was wrong again
What gives a person the right to treat him as they do?
For five years his life has been turned upside down
From pillar to post he's been pushed, no love has he found -
Too young to understand what he has done wrong
He just knows it won't be long
Why does the person who should have loved him the most
Scarred and disfigured him, looked through him like he's a ghost?
Only a child, no mind of his own, he knows no future happiness
                                                                     lies at home

He has to escape, he doesn't know how
He weeps and asks anybody to take away the pain
Make me feel like a boy again
Stop robbing me of my childhood
Stop hurting me inside
Let me be free, I've nowhere left to hide
I've tried to understand Dad how you can hurt me this way
But my mind's not the same, so please just go away
Leave me alone to die, or let me be free
But whatever you do Dad
Stop abusing me.

A New Life Is Born

He opens his eyes
he looks around
What's that there?
What's that sound?
Who's the person holding me now?
Should I cry?
I don't know how
What's that familiar smell?
Whose is that friendly voice?
Should I be happy? Should I rejoice?
Why is it so bright here when it was so dark inside?
Should I stay here? Or should I hide?
Oh no here comes the rubber to fill my waiting mouth
Hey you remove it, I want it out
What's that smell drifting in the air? Is it me?
Or is it you over there?
Hey put my clothes on before I catch cold, give me a cuddle
Do as you're told
Tuck me up gently while I sleep for a while, and while you're at it
Get some rest too
Because when I'm older it will be hard to do
And even though inside it was safe and warm
I'd rather be on the outside close to my mum.

It's Time To Come Home

I close my eyes and slowly sink into my subconscious
Bringing forward memories that I have enjoyed and regretted
I firstly picture myself as a child lost and lonely
Always searching for something I could never have
Then as a teenager rebelling against everything
Experiencing the happiness of first love
As an adult making many mistakes, but at the same time learning
                                                                             many lessons
Then comes forward my most precious memory the birth of my children
Six little replicas of myself who will continue to exist long
                                                                             after I'm gone.
They taught me not only how to be a mother
But also to appreciate all the things I had in life
I have experienced love so strong, that my heart felt like it was
                                                                           breaking in two
And sadness so great that at times I felt like giving up
But I never did because I had to be strong for others
But now as I grow weak and tired from fighting for the things that
                                                                   I can no longer have
I hold onto my memories for these I can take with me
For at last I can say it's time for me to come home.

The Lost Soul

A lost soul, trapped within worlds, void of all feeling
No longer existing for itself
Only remaining in the lives of the loved ones left behind
On a journey too long to imagine, an end never arriving
As its quest it continues.

Maria Pelengaris

Maria Pelengaris was born in London in 1963 of dual parentage, her mother being English and her father Greek Cypriot. She is also a twin. At the age of eight she emigrated to Cyprus with her family where they lived until 1979, living through the 1974 war, which led to the division of the island. On returning to England in 1979 Maria completed her schooling before going on to do a mathematics and business degree at the London School of Economics. She graduated in 1984, then worked in the City for a time, but decided to change course and leave the City behind, at the height of Thatcherism. In 1987 Maria packed a suitcase and went travelling to Western Asia and the Middle-East. It was during this time that she discovered her love for writing poetry and prose. On returning from her travels, Maria commenced a career in the National Health Service where she trained as a mental health nurse, qualifying in 1991. Her experiences within this system have influenced some of her writing. Themes such as deprivation, loss and disempowerment. Since 1994 Maria has worked in out-patient settings, as a Nurse Manager, where she feels that patients are given more choice and responsibility in their care. Maria is also a qualified practitioner in Cognitive Analytic Therapy (CAT). She believes in the positive benefits of natural therapies and herself practises Reiki, the Japanese ancient system of hands-on healing. Committed to her own personal and spiritual growth which is reflected in her work, and inspired by dream work, the unconscious and the concept of time, Maria's current aim is to focus more of her energy towards creative writing. Personal interests include writing, travel, history, football, theatre and cinema, mythology and mysticism. Maria has had several poems published in anthologies since 1992.

Reality

The leaves are dead, cut with a knife
No more will they live a new life
They don't live long to want the things
I seem to yearn for when nothing life brings

I sit here, a prisoner in my room
Reality to me is as far as the moon
I live in a dream, in the clouds if you like
But soon I must face it or trouble will strike

There is no drop of sweetness spared
To those of us who have never dared
To reach out for love in an empty heart
For fear that we might have to part
From the ray of light we hoped to see
Since hope is better than reality

The sun may shine but like a star
It can never touch, it is too far
I must stop dreaming and living in fear
The world needs me, surely that's why I'm here
Perhaps if I try love will come to me
I just cannot turn my back on reality

Here's to tomorrow, my yesterdays are gone
I must not be afraid to make heard my song
A song of love, peace not war
There's enough sadness without making more
I must try to teach others not to be
Afraid to face reality

For You

It must have been hard for you all those years ago
I can only imagine for I can never truly know
Were you a lonely and frightened child, my love
Feeling the hurt and pain as you tried to rise above

Did you ever wonder what you had done wrong
To be without your mother's love, to have to be so strong
A little child should know the power of security
And know someone is there, even for eternity

But now after so many years I still see pain in your eyes
Afraid to want something good in life, afraid to criticise
For will the past come back to haunt you? Best leave it alone
Best put on a brave face, don't want others to see you moan

Yet you were only a child, you did nothing wrong
You couldn't have known that then, you deserved to belong
And there is a place for you here on this Earth
Don't let anyone tell you different or bring down your self-worth

It's time to forgive yourself and let the self-hatred cease
Let go of the guilt, it is undeserved, let it be released
Feel the rage for all that you did not have back then
For all who treated you badly, all you wish to condemn

But remember, these are your feelings, to others they can do no harm
Though kept within you they can, so maybe it's time to disarm
Feel what you feel for as long as you need, my love
Then you will be free and I'll watch you fly as high as a dove.

A Moment In Time

As the rocks stood firm beneath the cloudless sky
I watched as nature took its course
But still the question first and foremost was, why?
Why burden us with such remorse

For just today you were here
Visiting this Earth to view its splendour
Then a moment in time saw your visit ended
That moment I will always remember

We fought a losing battle
As your line with life slowly slipped
Our selfish motives were to keep you
But fate had the stronger grip

Amongst the many shapes of rocky formations
And amidst the mountains I could but see
Endless streams feeding the dry, thirsty ground
And oh, in such pleasing harmony

These will stand the test of time
Long after our sun has dimmed
And though tears blurred my vision
I accepted that your cup of life had reached its brim

Now That I Love You

Now that I love you
What do I do with this love
For you are not here to love me
So what do I do with this love

It is too heavy for my shoulders to carry
And my body aches from the ravages of its pain
Maybe I ask too much of you
To relieve me from the confines of these chains

Now that I feel like a little child
Craving for someone to love me
What do I do with this craving
For you are not here to love me

I could think of our love as spiritual
Then there would be less need for your touch
But no matter how many times I may tell myself
This child needs to hold you so much

BLACK DREAM, BLACK DAY

That night I had a dream so vivid and so real
Alive with death, devoid of all appeal
Tonight I remember it as I did then
And hope that such a night will not be mine again

Motionless bodies draped in black, all in disarray
Black as the darkest night of an arctic winter's day
A tragic scene took place as if to be in slow motion
And I was a mere witness to the cause of painful emotion
Amongst the scattered debris came a figure dressed in white
Gracefully gliding, hopelessly searching for one who was not in sight

When do dreams become nightmares, I wonder
When they frighten in the dark like the roar of thunder
But there were no tears of sweat, no screams for the night to hear
No clear evidence to display my nocturnal fear
Instead clouds of consciousness appeared as images faded
And such was my relief that these visions had been traded

That night I had a dream I wondered what could mean
And in the morning I was a mere witness to a tragic scene
Nightmare or dream, it doesn't matter which one
For I wish you had stayed a fantasy and left me with the morning sun

All I Remember

It's easy to forget the loves that I've known
When feelings didn't count for much, emotions never shown
To sometimes feel so lonely in a crowded room
When departing from familiar faces never seemed too soon

It's easy to forget the words never spoken
When gestures of love were merely a token
Of the gratitude felt when comfort was given
And unexplained moods always forgiven

It's easy to forget desires that were hidden
With dormant dreams unstirred and broken hearts forbidden
But how I remember words that seemed so unkind
As they echoed and echoed in the caves of my mind

Now winter sets in to darken my days
Confusions, disillusions guide me into a maze
Oh how crazy are the nights filled with dreams
The tossing and turning in tormenting scenes

Though the passing of time causes memories to fade
And with it each season's colour changes in shade
There are thoughts in my mind of chances I've thrown
And all I remember are the loves that I've known

THE INCUBATION PERIOD

This is the time to heal,
The time to conceal
Oneself away from the outside
World.
Time to go within
And not be afraid
To face
The unknown.
There is a stranger you do not know,
Yet must.
The stranger will guide you to places
You would rather not see,
For you would rather not be
The things he says you are,
The things you said
You would never be.
Befriend the stranger
And his power ceases to be
The potent force
That has been unknown
To you,
Until now.
Know his power to be yours
Instead,
And you will learn to lose
Your fear of it
And of others.
Then you will know
The time of healing to have truly begun,
And slowly will it propel you
To venture back into the outside world
Where your living can be done.

Blood Sisters

Sister, sweet sister
with whom I've been blessed,
Your gentleness and your loveliness
my world you have caressed.

Throughout the days
the seasons and the years,
We've fought, we've loved
and we've shed our tears.

And with all this
we are more than sisters of the same name,
For the bond that holds us together
cannot be pictured and framed.

But then again, we started our life together
inside our mother's womb,
From no more than a tiny egg
that split quite perfectly into two.

And long before we viewed
the outside world and all its trouble,
We grew so slowly and gently
inside our warm water bubble.

And when the bubble burst
and we started our journey to the outside,
In getting there first, I had no choice
I didn't mean to push aside.

Then as you became so weak and so frail
they took you away for a while,
Only several years later did I realise
that I might never have seen your smile.

But you were given back to me
and together we continued to grow,
The life I almost faced alone
how thankful I was never to have to know.

And now that we have grown up
and live our separate lives,
There are others who have
become special in our eyes.

But remember, sweet sister
and please never doubt,
Your gentleness and your loveliness
I could never do without.

JOURNEY ON

I came to you with doubts and fears
One bright September morn
As I drove through those cold, iron gates
I entered a home in which I did not belong

What was I doing here?
I wasn't quite sure
Just a vague notion
That others' problems I could help cure

'Sorry you're leaving,' they said
When the time had come to break free
And to someone with self-esteem so humble
They uttered those words to me

So I left you with hopes for tomorrow
One dull December eve
And as I drove through those cold, iron gates
I knew I had found something in which I could believe.

TAJ MAHAL

You stand alone, majestic and strong
Worlds apart from the squalor around
You are the pearl in a sea of darkness
A sea where all hope has drowned

Your cold marble stone remains untainted with time
The same fate human hearts have not known
You have fascinating shades at dusk and at dawn
Though dirty dullness is the colour of your home

Your structure can seem symmetrical and plain
Yet to gaze at your beauty I would not tire
For one who expected such disappointment
What deep arousing feelings you did inspire

For many a year you have stood with pride
Powerfully drawing us under your spell
But behind your bold exterior of intrigue
A story of sensitivity you have to tell

A monument of love from one man to his wife
Her death oh how he did mourn
She who carried his fourteenth child
Then gave her life when it was born

Upon this story there are those who have frowned
Perhaps such sensitivity they could not abide
And though their hearts may be cloaked in cynicism
This was love there was no wish to hide

Six O'Clock

This is indeed the darkest hour
Of wicked thoughts and torturous dreams
Which inspire the soul
To rip to pieces
The drudgery and gloom
Of misspent youth.

Cast aside your wanton desires
The greed that embraces you,
And throw them into the well of deepest despair
Where a thousands voices will swallow you.

Your voice is unheard
Above the cacophony of frenetic visions
When once your voice was louder
Than the subordinates you 'ruled'.

Where do you go to now?
For pride is a hollow virtue.
There is but one way to go
For now is the darkest hour
As the clock face shows,
Its hands all but smirking
As you resign yourself
To finding friendless faces
In everything you see.

Marcella Pellow

I was born 75 years ago in a lovely house in Hampshire. Looking back on the upward path I have had to travel - often alone - I think there were some unkind auspices at birth. Childhood was golden - the lovely garden was heaven on earth to a four year old. I was a very talented child and gained the London Matric at 15. At the outbreak of war I was sent to my aunt's farm near Falmouth. I learned how to milk and loved all outdoor work. But the manic-depression I have suffered all my life descended on me. I was sent to a mental hospital for many months. At last, freedom once more and 'back to the land.' Foolishly, I left to become a nurse and had another relapse in the Blitz. Later I met Peter, an artist, and we married. It was a fiasco and I was deserted - nearly penniless - to rear our three beautiful children. I coached them all the way to the 11+, now they are all doing well. The eldest, Jane, is a Professor of Psychology.

Peter was unfaithful and finally, I left oxford (Wytham Abbey) to come 'home to mother' in Cornwall.

Later, I met Ben in his little holding 'Carloose', my heart's desire with the old clob cottage and cattle in the byre. We have now been married for 25 years and in spite of my recurring illness, life is idyllic. He is my standby and greatest friend.

Poetry has always been for me a vocation and relief in stress. Mother nature is my inspiration - I love all things green - also the sea in stormy weather, and my beloved family. Most of my writing comes from church guidance and I am influenced by Isiah, Revelations and all the New Testament.

God has been so good to me though I am now a widow.

GOOD FRIDAY

For our transgression crucified
The Son of Man has surely died.
On His head the thorny crown
While tears, like blood, flow mingled down.

Was no-one there to hear His cry
Lifted to our God on high?
'Why hast Thou forsaken me?'
In agony upon the tree.

He died, with thieves on either side
The gates of death were open wide.
Yet now He lives and reigns above
To hear our heartfelt cries of love.

EASTER

Christ who left the realms on high
To live with us, for us to die
That anguished cry upon the tree
'My God, has Thou forsaken me?'

He died for our iniquity
With His life he made us free -
He conquered death and lives on high
Risen that man no more may die.

The empty tomb, so long ago
Is proof our Saviour loves us so.
Great Shepherd, keep us by Thy side
Be Thou our only shield and guide.

Good Friday

Alone, in dark Gethsemane
Jesus wept and prayed for me.
Forsaken by those He loved the most
But guarded by the angel host.

Holy One, to Thee I pray
Send Thy grace to me today -
Let me learn to heed Thy voice
To make my wayward heart rejoice.

Christ who walked to Calvary
To give His life upon the tree.
For our sins He paid the price
With His supreme sacrifice.

Thankfulness

Gracious God, most holy Lord
Thy people's succour and reward
From beyond the realms of grace
Grant us a vision of Thy face.

Now the daylight fills the skies
Let my earth-born soul arise
To make my morning sacrifice.

Outside the earth is fresh and sweet
Such grass so green beneath our feet,
For all Thy gifts so freely given
We lift our hearts to Thee in heaven.

Three in one and one in three
Holy, holy Trinity.

To Our King Emmanuel

Let me her the age-old story
How Jesus Christ the king of glory
Left His Father's home on high
To live with us, for us to die.

Everywhere we see His power -
The beauty of the wayside flower,
The crescent moon alone in space
Gives us a vision of His face.

How we long to hear His voice
To make our anxious hearts rejoice,
We kneel to thank Emmanuel
Who came to Earth, with us to dwell.

Holy Shepherd, love divine
Come to this weak heart of mine.
With great compassion lead us on
To the place where Thou hast gone.

The Sea

The sea - the ever moving sea
Brought freshness to my soul.
The grace of God came unto me
His wonders made me nearly whole.

The music of the rolling waves
Now breaking on the shore.
The call of seabirds overhead
Bring God's mercy ever more.

Almighty One, I bow to Thee
To thank Thee for Thy loving care,
With great compassion come to me
I see Thy grandeur everywhere.

A Prayer For Grace

Spirit of wisdom, truth and love
Come to me from the realms above.
With Thy own unfailing grace
Give my wandering soul a place.

Here at dawn I kneel to Thee
O send compassion unto me.
When my Earthly hopes are dim
I pray my path will lead to Him.

Holy Jesus, day by day
Guide me surely on my way.
When the upward path is steep
Be the shepherd of Thy sheep.

For My Father

My Father, you have travelled
So far beyond the stars
But God's mercy has no boundary
His love has got no bars.

My Father, on your natal day
I pray that you will come once more
I long to feel your strong, right hand
Come through the ever-open door.

But if you never can come back
Listen to your daughter's prayer.
The little child you loved so much
Says thank you for your loving care.

Prayers Morn And Night

In the early morning
I kneel to Thee and pray -
Spirit of the living God
Be with me this day.

Late, at gentle eventide
The work and labour past
I know the Christ was at my side
The peace of God has come at last.

Crescent moon shining
With stars in the sky.
The symbols are sent
From the Saviour on High.

How can we give thanks
For this unfailing care?
His power and His love
Are abroad everywhere.

Spring Son

Holy Jesus, breathe on me
Speak to me in accents clear -
When the upward path is steep
Let me know that Thou art near.

Surely, surely, Spring is here
We see such beauty everywhere,
Pale blossom on the apple tree
It is the springtime of the year.

Lord of all things great and small,
God whose love is over all,
Keep us ever by Thy side
We need not fear with Thee beside.

Spring In Cornwall

O come to Cornwall in the spring
To see the trees all blossoming
Everywhere is fresh and sweet
With grass so green beneath our feet.

In the springtime of the year
The fragile bluebells now appear
Down the lane the wayside flowers
Delight our eyes in passing showers.

And all around the sparkling sea -
White waves breaking on the shore -
The calling seagulls overhead
Such beauty is for ever more.

The God of nature sends these gifts
With all the joy his love imparts
So let us kneel with outstretched hands
And offer up our humble hearts.

For The Milkman

Our milkman always makes the day
Rain or shine, he'll always say,
'Good morning sir, and how are you?'

This cheerful greeting drives away
The gloom of every winter day -
His friendliness and happy smile
Make the dreary chores worthwhile.

The milk is always by the door
And even if we ask for more
The daily pinta's always there
So, thank you milkman, for your care.

Garden In May

Pale blossom on the apple tree,
White daisies in the grass -
Blue speedwell scattered all around
God's love will never pass.

Here before the break of day
Such silence fills my soul
Beseechingly I kneel and pray
'Great Shepherd make me whole.'

I kneel to thank Thee for the spring
Which fills our hearts with joy.
Almighty Father, God and King
Let Thy praise our lips employ.

Christmas

Lo within the manger lies
He who made the starry skies
He who Heaven and Earth has wrought
And with His blood mankind has bought.

In that stable, rude and lowly
Came to us the child most holy -
Now we celebrate that birth,
The Son of God is born on Earth.

In the manger, on the hay,
The holy child has come today.
While angels Christmas anthems sing
We bow our heads to Christ, the King.

'CARLOOSE' (ONCE MY HOME)

Teddy bear, my teddy bear,
I wonder if you are aware
Of just how much I really care?

In those green field of long ago
'Twas there I learned to love you so -
That love has never gone away
Though many times I fall and stray.

'Carloose', my oft recurring dream
The meadows and the sparkling stream
The friendly byre and cottage small -
The peace of God was over all.

Alas those days will come no more
yet still I see the open door,
Where everywhere was fresh and sweet
With grass so green beneath our feet.

But now we have to wander on
Those magic days are past and gone
When love came in, a love profound
As dawn which breaks without a sound.

Trudy Lapinskis

I am 38 years old, have RSD which is Reflex Sympathetic Dystrophy for which, at present, there is no cure and I live my daily life in a wheelchair in constant pain. My outlet to the outside world as I'm virtually house-bound apart from going to the hospital, is my poetry where I can put into my words about the pain I suffer and give thanks to the people who've helped me so much, my gran who has looked after me since I was twelve and given me great strength. also my specialist, Dr John Wedley from London Bridge Hospital and Guys, whom I found through a lot of searching and has been my one hope to help with the pain where others failed. Also his secretary, Mrs Maureen Cooper who's also made me laugh and got me into treatment as soon as possible, also all the nurses at the above hospital who have kept me cheerful and become my friends. Without these people, my life would be very depressing, but my poetry has changed all that and I can thank them all. Also, my inspiration has been my grandfather, father and brother, who've all been in the armed forces and this topic of remembrance I've included in my poetry, plus children of war. I can express my feelings through my poetry and also remember wonderful people I've met in hospital who've now passed away. I also hope my poetry will reach out to those people in pain and grief and help them cope with it a little easier. Also, I've written poems about the two most wonderful people who've been in our world, Princess Diana and Mother Teresa.

RSD is quite a rare condition, not in America where six million people have it, but the more people know about it, the more research can be done in this country and then we're not behind the rest of the world where there are about 100 research centres, including one in Beirut whilst a war's been going on. So my experience of RSD and hospitals and nurses may help others not to be afraid. While helping to raise awareness about RSD, I would lastly like to thank Professor Povlsen and his wife, his secretary, my latest consultant who has straightened my badly deformed fingers.

MY BROTHER GARRY

This is a poem written especially for my brother,
To me, there couldn't possibly be another,
He's always been there for me through good times or bad,
Life with him around is never dull or sad,
We're more like twins because we're only 18 months apart,
This could be one of the reasons why he'll always be in my heart,
Life hasn't always been a bowl of cherries, my mum moving him away when he was ten,
He later joined the army where they turn boys into men,
Then a few years later the call came to say he wanted to come home,
At last we would be back together and I would be no more alone,
Life wasn't easy for him to adjust for a start,
He'd been looked after by the army and we'd all been so far apart,
I've since become disabled but he's always there for me,
He's one of life's special caring people you see,
I know he'll protect me and never let me come to any harm,
Always resolving a situation and remaining calm,
I'll always love him from the bottom of my heart,
And this from his older sister may we never have to part,
Life picked up for him since he met a lady named Claire,
She gives him love he should have had as a child and now life seems a lot more fair,
If I had the money I'd make his dreams come true and buy him a Formula 1 car,
So you never know Garry your dreams may come true, just keep wishing upon a star,
Don't ever change because you're so special as you are,
A brother in a million Garry is what you are.

Jackie

This is a poem dedicated in the memory of my friend Jackie,
She was a fun-loving person, made everyone laugh, sometimes wacky,
When I was in hospital and very scared,
Her caring kindness to me, she shared,
I was having my first operation and on my own
But Jackie and her sister never once made me feel alone,
Whenever I went down to London they would be there,
Now Jackie's been taken away from us it's just not fair,
She was young, full of life and full of personality,
Why she should be taken away from us I cannot see,
For all the help and love she's given to others God must need her there
It's a pity it had to be now, when so few people in the world care,
God must want her by his side,
So in him now she can confide,
Here on earth she had so much love,
Now she's gone to be an angel up above,
When I think of her I can't help but shed a tear,
But at times I feel she's next to me or very near,
In our memory she'll remain forever,
Forget her is something we cannot do not never,
So God, please look after her for us, and hold her hand,
So we can rest in the knowledge she's gone to a better land,
She was truly one of the nicest people I've met,
So Jackie, my friend, who gave so much I never will forget.

MOTHER TERESA

This lady gave her life to the homeless, dying, needy and sick
Who done everything she could to change their lives brick by brick
When no one else was there
This remarkable lady was always the one to care,
Mother Teresa was their shining light,
When everything around was dim, not bright,
They were helpless, out there all alone,
Until Mother Teresa took them in and gave them a home,
She gave up all her material things,
To help anyone whatever their sins,
When the calling from God came,
She was there, and life for her would never be the same,
To this lady the whole world owes so much,
But at last now it's God's hands she will touch,
She lived her life to work for God,
Along a weary and often difficult path she trod,
But Mother Teresa now rest in peace,
The good work you've done will never cease,
You were here to show others the way
And the sisters of missions will continue today,
You surely do now deserve a rest,
Out of all the people in this world, you were one of the best,
So now as you walk through heaven's open door,
You take with you all our love and more,
You truly were the mother a lot of people never had,
Turning their hearts around from sad to glad,
So thank you Mother Teresa for all you've ever done,
You deserve to be made a saint, because you were the chosen one.

Dr Wedley

I'm forever grateful for what you do,
Because doctors knowing about RSD are very few,
When I couldn't find anyone to help me with this pain,
I somehow found you because doing normal things I have to abstain,
The pain makes the days seem long, but the nights longer,
You've given me strength to help me feel stronger,
The trust I have in doctors are few,
But my complete trust I have in you,
I know there is no cure, and the pain sometimes I have to endure,
But I'll be forever grateful of that I'm sure,
You do your best to help my quality of life improve,
To take away some of the pain and make my everyday life run more smooth,
I'm eternally grateful and thanks for all you've done,
It's like a light at the end of a tunnel or the morning sun,
It's thanks to you, I can go on, hoping to get rid of the pain and really live
So all my heartfelt wishes to you I give.

Time

Time is like a clock ticking in your heart,
It beats to the sound of tic, toc, tic, toc.
It has no start, or no end,
It stretches on into the distance, completely invisible,
Our lives revolve around time, appointments we have to keep,
Wakes us up in the morning and the last sound we hear before sleep.
Without a clock, we can still tell the time,
The sky tells us if it's night or day,
The seasons tell us the time of year,
It's there in our every moment, but unlike us it never stands still,
We cannot step back in time, it has no reverse,
Only goes forward and we have to follow,
What's in the future, we do not know,
Time holds the key, so we'll just have to wait and see.

NHS

What is happening to the NHS?
It's falling down and in distress,
The doctors and nurses are overworked and underpaid,
Patients expecting an operation only to be told it's been delayed,
The waiting lists grow and grow,
For any operation from your head down to your toe,
Where will the money come from they say?
But your life is too high a price to pay.
Life is precious and the elderly need more care,
Leaving them to suffer just isn't fair,
As technology increases, demand for care is greater,
What conclusions are there from the increased data?
There's no time to waste, funding is needed today.
We have to stop the ward closures without delay,
Patients can't be left on trolleys in the corridor,
The NHS is a free service to help the poor,
We'd all give a little to stop this rot,
It's time to do something that to us all means a lot,
We have to help the NHS to survive,
After all it keeps us healthy and alive!

A Child Of War

The child's body lay on the ground a shallow empty shell,
The nightmare over a release from this living hell,
His days filled with guns, bombs and war,
No parents to love him, no one to adore,
He'd lost them long ago, left alone to survive,
Killing others, doing anything he had to, to stay alive,
The days and nights were dark for him everyday,
No chance, to make friends go out and play,
He's now gone to a place where others have gone before,
At last he'll be welcomed through an open door,
He'll find peace as God lays his hand upon his head,
He's at rest, no more worries now he's dead,
Gone now to a far better place,
Frown lines, sadness and tears disappear from his face,
Ours is not to reason why,
Young, innocent children die,
He'll be laid to rest in an unmarked grave,
His life we were unable to save,
But this child's life was not in vain,
If in the future from wars we do abstain.

Remembrance Day

The poppies flutter down from way up high,
To form a sea of red blood on the ground they lie,
Each one for a man or woman who died,
A chance of longer life they were denied,
These were the brave, unsung heroes lost in time,
They went to war, alone, youthful, fit and in their prime,
As we stand on this cold, damp, grey day,
For our lost family, who fought for us we pray,
They trudged through battle, weary, exhausted and forlorn,
Fighting for the country, where they'd been born,
To make our world a better place to live in today,
For this price, their lives they had to pay,
Forever in our hearts they will be,
Until the day, we'll join them, and their face we'll see,
The sound of the bugler, playing the last post,
Silence is everywhere, is that my father, son, no it's a ghost,
The horrors of war, can never be forgotten, so we remember them
Standing tall, poppy in lapel, we salute to the National Anthem,
Not just today, but every day, we'll hold them dear,
Locked forever in our hearts they'll always be near.

Pain

The pain is always there, it won't go away,
How I wish I could be free of it for just one day,
It nags and gnaws and stabs and shoots
As though I've been kicked by huge black boots,
When I move about the pain increases,
It's always there and always displeases.
When will someone help with this pain,
From doing normal things I have to abstain,
The days seem long, but the nights are longer,
I try and do exercises to make me stronger,
The pain is cold, it's sometimes hot,
But no one seems to know what I've got.
For me it's something I always feel,
It's bigger than me and very real,
But this pain won't get me beat,
I'll fight on till I can get on my feet.
When you give in the pain has won,
It's then got you continuously on the run,
So I'll stand still and put up a fight,
For what I believe in, it is my right,
There's always someone much worse off than me,
So I'll beat this pain, I will, you'll see.

With Thanks

Before I lay my head down to sleep,
I pray to the Lord my soul he'll keep,
I thank you Lord for each day you give,
Keeping me alive, and helping me to live,
I've put my faith in you, so whatever you decide,
I will accept because Lord by you I will abide,
There are times of joy and times of sorrow,
With each passing day then comes tomorrow,
I know you're always there by my side,
Whichever path you've chosen for me I cannot hide,
You give me strength and love because you care,
So that my love for others I will then share,
I know when the time comes you'll send for me,
You'll hold me in your arms and your face I'll see,
Any sadness and sorrow I've had will disappear,
Because in your kingdom I'll have nothing to fear,
So I'll thank you for everything you've given me,
I know that what will be, will be,
You've given me this precious gift of life,
And you're there to hold my hand through trouble and strife,
I'll smile and be thankful for what I've got,
Your love, faith and trust in me means a lot,
All my love to you, I'll send in this prayer,
From the moment I was born you've always been there,
So if I should die before I awake,
I ask you Lord if my soul you'll take.
Amen.

WHY SHOULD WE BE SO SCARED OF THE DARK?

As I go out at night and gaze up at the sky,
I look at the moon and stars way up high,
What is out there exactly we do not know,
If there's aliens are they friend or foe?
The blackness of the night fills us with fear
But if they're aliens watching us they're not here,
Why should we be so scared of the dark?

The stars are twinkling shining brightly,
Like thousands of diamonds, sparkling in a cluster tightly,
We'd like to reach out our hand, the stars to hold,
But they're too valuable worth more than gold,
It's the things that we can't see we fear the most,
Could we have had a hallucination, or was it a ghost?
Why should we be so scared of the dark?

Our hearts beat faster we feel a chill,
Shivers creep up our spine, everything's so still,
Not a sound to be heard, it feels so cold,
This has to be all in our mind, so we're told.
The cemetery's spooky,
The church bells are ringing,
The wind is whistling, or is it singing?
Why should we be so scared of the dark?

Joanna L Hammond

I was born in 1980 and grew up in a town called Bexleyheath, where I now begin my adulthood. I went to school here and later moved on to Greenwich University where I am currently studying a computer HND.

I was first inspired to write poetry by a close friend who had attempted a very successful poem packed full of emotion which moved many people. I saw how easily words could turn into feeling and I attempted my first poem at the age of fifteen.

English was always a subject I enjoyed and progressed with and I went on to study it at A Level. It was at this time I began to take a stronger interest in poetry and learnt to perceive a strong impression of the writer from his/her style of writing. I realised that it can be possible to express words in such a passionate and clever way.

My main interests are reading, writing my poetry and of course, socialising with friends. I read books which are packed full of philosophy which I find extremely interesting, and also subjects related to dreams and spiritual aspects.

Nowadays I am inspired strongly by what I see or feel. I write many of my poems after I have experienced a certain rush of emotion be it happy or sad. My poetry does not follow any particular theme as many are from personal experiences or ones I have witnessed. Perhaps the only poem which carries a theme is 'An Eternal Ocean Dream'.

I hope to continue writing poetry for many years as I believe it is something I will always enjoy and never forget how to do, as no one is ever free of emotion.

A Summer's Afternoon

As the sun sifts through the trees
I feel its heat bounce off my pale skin
Retracting back into the wide curve of blue above
The birds chirp merrily from the looming branches
And the bees buzz happily through the sombre breeze
With flowers stretching their coloured necks high
To catch the warmth as it drifts on by.

A small red beetle lands upon my arm
With dots of white glowing with charm
It tramples over the jungle of my arm
Completely fearless of what may do it harm
I feel its soft tickling feet tread my bare skin
Until a sudden breeze sweeps him off his feet
He floats through the air without a care
Until he is deposited onto a flower across the garden so bare.

Love Is . . .

Sometimes love's a river
Sometimes love's a chain
Sometimes it causes nothing but pain.
But I say love is a flower
With a growing seed to spread
And with this love brings power
Which fills my once lonely head.
Let's keep love forever
Let's keep it in our hearts
For one day it could turn sour
And we could be lonely parts.
But if sometimes love is like a river
And never like a chain
Then the flower should still blossom
Until our dying day.

UNTITLED

If a bird had the chance to walk not fly
If a whale had the chance to be so dry
Would they all try and would they know why?
If a child had either a stick or stone
Which would he choose, which would do more harm?
If an orphan had to laugh or cry
Which would he choose and would he know why?
If that child then had a chance or a certainty
What would he choose, which could he love
Would it be right or it be wrong?
Would it be clever, would it be strong?

Just a chance at life is what makes it real
Not what it could have been
Not what they could maybe or used to feel.
If the bird had his choice it would be to fly
If the whale had his choice he would not be dry
What they are is final and not to be changed
What they are is happy and grateful not blamed
If the child chose the stick he could do harm
Just the same if he had chosen the stone
But to do without made him better still
As his life after certainty would definitely be real.

Our lives are not chosen by others close by
We dictate them ourselves, with guidance we still try
If we all had a stick or a stone, even both
We would be no different we could not boast
To make it real is to do just what we feel
It all goes bad when we think what we could have had
But the bird and the whale are happy in naiveté
Of a life they could have chosen with such greed
But they didn't even recognise a need

To swim and to fly is them and their life
So be you and yourself, it can't change like the wind
Others have worse, others have better
To make yourself one you have to try harder
The bird doesn't wonder and wish so hard
The whale doesn't tamper, regret and discard
The answer to life is not a gift we have to earn
It's what we already have without trying at all.

A Haze Of Memory

I wander amongst the huge yellow sunflowers
The lazy haze sets off a mirage of entwining figments
I see you both travelling on your eternal journey
As the sun billows down on my dream

I could still spot you in a room full of crowded people
Each one holding onto a separate ominous destination
You both absent mindedly merge into a cluster of figmentation
Disturbed only by the landing of a busy bee

This transparent image leaves a series of memories
Each one has its own place in my heart
As they float through my soul giving wisdom and love
The pain is drifting into this place above

Confusion turns to wonder as the heartache is understood
And the messages come together; you were happy in this world
So I take a bright yellow petal and hold it to my face
It is a part of you both and will always keep this place

AN ETERNAL OCEAN DREAM

Our journey began in a tranquil sea
Which endured the over now resting in me.
With differing memories and reverent affection
Love was finally brought about in the right direction.
Wandering through mild ecstasies of narcotical waves
I felt something float heavily within and settle upon my heart.
I soon discovered through my depth of feeling
That I could at last experience solitude with a real meaning,
For to fear love is to fear life itself.

Veiled in mystery our journey continues
After surviving a wave of anguish and sometimes fear,
We have a beginning which now becomes clear.
For the sea is calm now your love surrounds it
Just as my heart felt joy when you at last came to find it.
Now I just want you to really know
That our love can begin to thrive and grow.

As the sky rushes with warm white clouds
I look up from within the calming depths
And I see old memories are at last set free
Then lost within the screaming sea.
For when I think of love as something powerful and new,
I think of it as something I want to share with just you.
As we drift along with the current of life
We now finally reach the shore which can end all our strife.
For when I'm in your arms nothing seems to matter
You've won this place in my heart,
You've won my Ocean Dream.

Pain

The things that cause the hurt,
Are never known.
Deep down inside
Is something true,
But always blind.

No one knows how to stop the pain,
It's always there.
Without a frame it cannot be caught,
It's left free to cause the hurt.

Who understands how I feel,
No one knows.
They may pretend,
But the hurt still grows.

There may be a time, a certain place
Where someone will find a dream to replace
The one I lost when the hurt arrived
The one I dreamt which never survived.

Where it went I do not know,
Will it come and take back the pain
I need to know.

I'll always remember the times we had before
Before it came and took my love
Then crushed it to the floor.
Why does pain hurt so bad
There's nothing left inside to explain
Why the dream had to leave my side.

Untitled

Capture happiness in a deep long frame
Keep it locked passionately inside the human heart
Save old memories for that rainy day
For what tomorrow brings one cannot say

Don't waste time on jealous hearts
Your choices you make are already half chance
The world will continue to speak through paper lips
But the sober truth will always remain

Do not be afraid of duration of time
Instead help witness the inconceivable number of stars
As their cold silver fire drips from their corners
Hiding now the blackened blaze of sun

As it sifted through the trees
We hide away in a from full of feeling
Just like the sun hides from prying hands and unwanted changes
Which face it daily with such wisdom and style

We slowly merge with the shadow of life
As it makes contact with our endless pale complexion
The definite shape soon softens
Protecting us from the hidden truth within

Its texture now bringing comfort and warmth
As it makes contact now calming all roughened edges
Its abstract personality lies still; it listens
But can return no reply

Knowing faithfully only man is able to cry
Unable to detest a single tear, or fear any fear
It is us who are the wise and powerful
And them who are unfound and vulnerable

Wallowing in confinement still lies a burning desire
To dissolve into what now surrounds us
To leave no trace behind our journey
Just an honest but lonely life to find.

ONE DAY

Some day I'll reach that river
Which flows with ideas to follow
Each day I get that little bit further
Until a barrier sets up in front of me.

I haven't got the strength to break it
My heart is too weak
I only wish I had the power
To get up and speak.

It reaches out with inviting arms
But they are too short to touch me
I'm stuck in the distance
Just a vague memory.

Maybe if I sit and wait
There's a chance it will reach me first
I do not know all its powers
Mine I know are too weak.

Until I'm sure of what to do
I will build up my strength
Then one day
I'll get there, I'll reach that river.

LONELY

Lonely inside the feelings are trapped
No one to talk to I'm all alone
My head spins with emotions
Each one waiting to burst.

Outside is clear and bright
I stay in fearing the unknown
Only the four walls surrounding keep me
I stay in hiding.

Someone come and set me free
I send out a message
The answers just bounce off the walls
I still sit waiting to be relieved
I still sit in my own world.

How I long to have a clear mind
But what you did to me made me blind
I cannot see past my window
Where a world waits to be filled.

How long do I have to wait
For someone to come
Maybe a day
Maybe forever
Until then my four walls keep me safe.

MICK WEBSTER

My name is Mick Webster, and I am forty-two years old. I am married with five children, and two beautiful granddaughters. I was born in Blackpool, and later lived for a short while in Canada, and then for six years in America, before returning to England, where I met my lovely wife - Eileen. I now live in the picturesque town of Market Drayton, in Shropshire, where I am the manager of an amusement arcade.

I get quite a surprised reaction from people, when they find out that I write poetry. But nevertheless, I have received some positive comments about my poems. With my shaven head, tattoos, and earrings, I suppose that I don't look as people expect a poet to.

I like my poems to come from the heart, and find my poetry, a good way of expressing my thoughts, and views, be they serious or otherwise.

If when someone reads one of my poems, and shows some emotion, then I've succeeded in what I set out to do.

I have only been writing for a couple of years, and have been encouraged all of the way, by my beautiful wife - Eileen.

Sometimes, with my poems, it is as if I am writing about memories, of events in past lives. Could we have lived other lives before now - I wonder?

In an increasingly stressful world, I find that writing down my thoughts, helps me to 'chill out', and find a calm, that otherwise, is missing from my life.

I hope that after reading some of my work, that hopefully you may want to, sample some more.

THE SKY IS FALLING

The time has come
For me to speak
Of shattered dreams
That once grew sweet

Of hopes, aspired
Treasures, unfound
It seems, the sky
Is falling down

Many dreams escaped me
Not meant to be
Can eyes be open
Yet, still not see

Ambitions, persued
Life, full circle, goes round
It seems, the sky
Is falling down.

HEAVEN'S ECHO

Sunlight tickling, calm, lazy waters
Trees, their leaves, slowly dancing, in the breeze
Blue skies, wiped clear of clouds
Birds, singing a serenade, of life
The day is calm, untroubled
Heaven's echo
Here on Earth

SUMMER'S BRIEF SONG

Strolling hand in hand
As the world goes by
On a carpet of green
Under blue electric sky
With songs of bird on the wing
Flying free, soaring high
Under clouds of angel hair
Set in clear summer sky
Trees speak of life
Garbed in green, standing proud
Flowers in full bloom
Standing silent, beauty loud
Nature in full abundance
Swathed in warmth of the sun
Before the season must turn
And dark winter next comes.

DARK BEFORE DAWN

In the dark fleeting hours before dawn
When sleep evades me
The images of the night have fled
The new day, not yet begun
My mind wanders near and far
In the tranquillity of the hour
This is the time I love the most
My thoughts flow free, unfettered
The silence is my host
Then, as the dawn does break
Heralded, by the birds in song
I lay, listening in my bed
Peaceful and sedate
Another day has just begun.

Daddy's Girl

It's a strange thing he endures
She's no longer Daddy's little girl it seems
Before his eyes, his daughter matures
Wanting to break away, now reaching her teens
Still, he wants to offer protection
To shelter her from harm
From youth that has gone wild
With false-fronted charm
With every attention shown from boys unknown
Alarm bells ring in his head
He knows he's over protective
But he feels, she's easily led
It's painful, but he must step back and wait
As she finds her own way in life
Still protective of his daughter
Even when she becomes a wife.

Mother And Daughter

All alone she sits
Alone with her memories
The sun glistening
As it catches, the tear in her eye
It's not a long-lost love, she mourns
But someone, so much more precious
Someone so special, that words cannot express
The bond between, a mother and her daughter
Not a day goes by, when she doesn't cry
Tears of sadness, but also tears of joy
For the life of the woman
Who was like no other
Her Mother

Painful Goodbyes

They took him to visit his brother
To the hospital, many miles away
He didn't know that his brother was dying
He just thought, he was going to play

Benny had lost all his long hair
And his thin arms had tubes going in
When little Tommy ran up to his bedside
His eyes opened, and he managed a grin

'Hi ya Tommy I'm feeling so poorly
I'm glad you came to see me today
Little brother, you know that I love you
But I think, soon, I'm going away'

Mum and Dad, both felt their hearts breaking
The tears, flowing free, in their eyes
Two little brothers, holding each other tightly
As if they were saying their goodbyes

One last sigh, and then Benny's grip loosened
He'd hung on, till little Tommy was near
His suffering done, it was over
In the corner of his eyes, was a tear

He'll never forget his big brother
Remembered every night in his prayer
He has a special love, for his Benny
That only two brothers can share

They go and put flowers on Ben's grave now
All of them, shedding a tear
Little Tommy sobs, 'Benny I love you'
And Benny knows his brother is near.

A House Filled With Love

Rooms once filled with laughter
Now filled with deafening silence
Walls that once echoed with love
Now strangely dumb
Yet the sounds of my childhood
Still abound in my mind
This house, which was once a home
Once watched and kept vigil
On a family, bonded with love
This house, now strangely silent
Abandoned, and forlorn
The very air, of its rooms
Seemingly, lacking in being
As if waiting, patiently
Till, once more
Happy, joyous, voices
Bring new life, to its fabric
This house, once was our home.

Ten Paces At Dawn

You Sir, have no manners
You are, I think, a cad
I demand some satisfaction
For your actions, they are bad

I throw the gauntlet down for you
I consider you with scorn
The matter we'll settle, in due course
A duel we'll fight, at dawn

Pick your pistol, then stand back to back
We'll then ten paces walk away
We shall settle it, in this fashion
For it is the gentlemen's way

The deed is done, the pistol smokes
And good has overcome bad
It was my bounded duty, Sir
For you Sir, were a cad.

A Penny For Your Thoughts

If I could see inside your mind
If I could read, your every thought
What mixed emotions, would I find
Would I discover, more than I ought
Your every dream, your very core
Every word you leave unsaid
Would I be surprised, by what I saw
By thoughts, inside your head
Could I stand the thoughts, of loves long past
Or would jealousy blur my view
Is it the uncertainty
Of things I never knew
Would I feel threatened, would I feel scared
By thoughts that I might find
And would I like what I had bared
If I could see inside your mind.

Chances Are

Chances are, that one day I'll be rich
Or, more to the point, that I won't
Chances are, that I really deserve it
Or more likely than that, that I don't

Chances are, by the Queen, I'll be knighted
For services rendered in life
Chances are, the only way that I'll get crowned
Is with a rolling pin, swung by my wife

Chances are, that I'll go down in history
A man known for his fortune and fame
Chances are, I am only a dreamer
And they won't even remember my name

Chances are, that when I'm dead and buried
That my genius at last, they will see
Chances are, they will look at my tombstone
Scratch their heads, and then say, who was he?

Broken Dreams

I've achieved a few things, in my lifetime
But a lot, has escaped me, it seems
Though I've always, had just good intentions
Welcome to my world, of broken dreams

I was sure, that one day, I'd be famous
But it just, didn't work out that way
I guess dreams were made to be broken
In a lifetime, as fragile as clay

I dreamt that the world would know peace
No more starving, or hurting, or tears
Just another dream, to be broken
I've dreamt away so many years

But still, I keep, hoping and praying
For contentment, and all that it means
But more often than not, it avoids me
Welcome, to my world, of broken dreams.

JOY OR SHAME?

Consider I ask you
If you may
How would you greet the Lord
If he came today?

Would you offer your hand
And a welcoming seat
Or fall in worship
At his feet?

Could you hold your head up
Dare to, look in his eye
Or be ashamed, of times gone by?

Would you beg forgiveness
Of sinful things
Or just bow your head
To the King of Kings?

Rhapsody Of My Eyes

Beauty surrounds me
If only I will see
Nature serenades me
So wonderful and free

I scarce can comprehend
The myriad, of wonder that I see
And it costs me, not a penny
It's mine, if I will see

The yellows, bright like sunshine
Greens, of the living leaf
The reds, like passion flaming
Browns, the earth beneath

What nectar, what sweet rapture
Let me drink it, with mine eyes
Let me see, what joy surrounds me
The Rhapsody, of my eyes.

Why?

Just a pub, full of people
A sight, known so well
Till a hidden bomb, turned it
To a vision, from hell

They left it, under a table
Then calmly, walked away
Many, innocent people
Maimed, and injured, that day

Why, must they do this
Why must they, cause death
Why must they, feel hatred
With each, living breath

We must, find a way, to stop this
In whatever, way we can
This abomination, in God's eyes
Man's inhumanity, to Man.

WHERE LIES THE BLAME?

What went wrong
Oh, child of mine
Should I have known
Have seen a sigh

Was it pressure from friends
Were you easily led
Is that, why I'm mourning
Is that, why you're dead

What made you choose
The lifestyle you did
You wanted the big time
I wanted my kid

I hope now, you're happy
And I hope now, you're free
Where does the blame lay
The blame, points to me.

Tina Rooney

My name is Tina Rooney and I was educated at Monkwearmouth Comprehensive school in Sunderland, the City of Sunderland College and the University of Sunderland, where I gained a BSc (Hons) in Energy Technology Management. Unfortunately, I am currently unemployed, but I am a voluntary IT tutor with Ability Training, training adults with learning and physical disabilities in IT skills and I live with my parents. I started writing poetry in 1995 as part of my grandad's epitaph and two years later I started entering poetry competitions and enjoyed doing them. Three of my poems have been published, these were Exams, Oh What A Bloody War! and Diana, Princess of Wales. After they were published, I was encouraged to do more. All of my poems are based on everyday life or world events. They are based on items that have happened to me or on the news.

OH WHAT A BLOODY WAR!

Oh What A Bloody War!
Marching for days on end.
Our feet blistered and sore.
Oh What A Bloody War!
For survival we built trenches.
When it rains, it drenches.
Oh What A Bloody War!
What was the purpose of this fighting law?
As we fought for country and Queen.
Our comrades dying, we had seen.
Oh What A Bloody War!
Was there no end to all this fighting?
As a soldier spotted another sighting.
The soldier, with his gun took aim.
With one shot, he made the enemy lame.
Oh What A Bloody War!
It was not over yet.
How I wanted to be home with my pet.
Oh What A Bloody War!
11 hour 11 month 11 day
How we felt, I could not say.
As it was Armistice Day!
Over the battlefield not a gun or grenade could be heard.
To young people today, it may sound absurd.
But it was the day the war had been won.
A new era had begun.
So let us not forget the past.
And make our memories last.
Not a word is said
As we stand silent for one minute.
To remember our glorious dead.
For those who survived.
They can now grow old.
For their stories have been told.

SHINING LIGHT

I see a shining light,
That stands out bright.
Unfortunately, I cannot stay,
I have to go away.
God, up above,
Please, look after those I love.
I have tried my best,
But God, you have put me to the test.
I have been in a lot of pain,
For my family, and myself it has been a strain.
I close my eyes,
And breathe my last breath and heave my last sighs.

Slowly as I die,
Please do not cry.
As you will always remember me,
And the days we walked through the Lea.
My body is at peace,
The pain, it has ceased.
As I walk into the shining light
That stands out bright.

SUNRISE, SUNSET

The sun rises in the morning.
The world is waking up yawning.
As a new day is dawning
It rises from the East.
As everyone is having breakfast and a feast
We all get ready for work and school.
Let us hope the day is not too hot, but cool.

Suddenly the day has ended,
It is time to go home.
On our way we will roam.
It is time for the sunset in the West.
As the birds return to their nest
It is time for the sunset to go down.
Behind the fields on the edge of town.

It is time for the moon to come out at night.
And the stars that shine bright.
It is time for us to go to bed and rest.
It is what we all do best.
Soon it will be time for a new day beginning.
As the cockerel crows,
And the church bells start ringing.

KOSOVO CHILD
(As told by a young child)

I am a Kosovo child.
So meek and mild.
My country is at war.
Walking long distances, has made my feet blistered and sore.
My clothes are torn and I have a dirty face.
As a child I know my place.
I cannot play on a child's slide.
Instead I have to run away and hide.
As a child, I do not understand.
But know this was once a green and pleasant land.

Some people travel by lorry.
The Serbs, they are not sorry.
They have taken my family away.
How I wanted them to stay.
Another bomb blast.
How long will this war last?

I try to think of nice thoughts.
It is the way I have been taught.
But all I can do is cry.
And wonder why.
Who will look after me?
And leave my country alone, let it be?
I have no water and food.
Who will feed my hungry brood?
Who will shelter me from the rain?
Who will ease my pain?
I put my hands together and pray.
Maybe one day we can return and stay?

My country has been destroyed, I can see.
NATO are helping out, they have answered our plea.
My people have done nothing wrong.
To boost moral, we sing a song.
My country grows colder.
I would like a future, for when I grow older.
For I am only a child.
So meek and mild.

JILL DANDO

Jill, you were so brutally killed.
The air, it was stilled.
You were killed with one shot to the head,
Our tears, we have shed.
You will be sadly missed by your colleagues from the news,
When you were on television, the viewers sat on pews.
For those who met you, you brought so much fun,
You were the presenter of Holiday, visiting countries with lots of sun.
You were fighting against crime,
Till the end of your time.
Your fiancé, Alan Farthing will notice someone missing,
He will be missing your hugs and kissing.
You and him should have been married,
Over the threshold, you would have been carried.
Let us hope your killer is caught,
Lessons in justice, he will be taught.
Sleep well Jill,
As your funeral approaches Weston-Super-Mare,
Members of the public stand and stare.
And the air is still.

GLOBAL WARMING

Global warming is very alarming.
The environment it is harming.
Caused by human beings
Dumping their waste.
They dump it anywhere in their haste.
Their cars causing fumes
As the New Year looms.
Bringing CO_2 into the air
It is just not fair!
Animals, plants and trees have died
Environmentalists, they have tried.
Earthquakes, hurricanes, tidal waves and floods
What is it after, our blood?
Houses and bodies swept away
Maybe if they were better prepared
They could stay.
Forest fires caused by the sun
It is not over yet, it has to be won.
So let us all work together to stop the pollution
And come up with a solution.
There is too much traffic on the roads
If the car were left at home, it would lighten the load.
It is time to keep fit and start to cycle on a bike
Or maybe you could take a hike.
If factories were to decrease their fumes
The smog would not loom
And all of the flowers would bloom.

The air, it would be clear
Away from global warming we would steer.

Tigers, elephants and polar bears would not be extinct.
It is just what makes people think.
The weather, it is changing
Gusts of wind up to 90mph are ranging.
Causing extreme damage
But if we all pull together, we will manage.
So let us try and save this earth
For all that Mother Nature is worth!

DIANA, PRINCESS OF WALES

As you lay dying in that fatal car crash,
A whole nation started crying.
As the news broke of that horrific smash,
The medical team tried their best,
But in the end they had to lay you to rest.
You touched the nation's heart,
As your marriage fell apart.
You cared for the two boys,
When they were young, you bought them toys.
You carried out so many good deeds,
Always helping those in need.
Take a bow Di,
As it is time to say goodbye.

Millennium

The millennium will soon be beginning.
Auld Lang Syne people will be singing.
Most people will be dancing on the disco floor.
While others will be first footing at the door.
But when we make our New Year resolutions
Think of people less fortunate and think of any solutions.
For example we could bring the homeless in from the cold
And please do not forget the old.
Redundancy and unemployment
For them they will be no enjoyment.
Think of those who fought for country and Queen.
Their comrades dying they have seen.
Think about the countries at war.
Their children's clothes battered and torn.
Teach your children about crime.
For the sake of old father time.
Teach them about drink and drugs.
As one day they may turn into thugs.
Think about third world countries with no water or food.
Who will feed their hungry brood?
Think about global warming.
The environment it is harming.
England has a Millennium Dome.
But what about those suffering at home?
Living all alone, with no one to talk to on the telephone.
Is it worth ringing out the old and bringing in the new?
As there are people wandering around with holes in their shoes.
We could put a stop to road rage.
As a new year starts, it is time to turn over a new page.
Let us make this world a better place.
For the sake of the human race.
It is time to put behind our fears.
And celebrate another century, so raise your glasses and shout cheers!